Collector's Progress
NEW REVISED EDITION

Also by Stanley W. Fisher

ENGLISH BLUE AND WHITE PORCELAIN OF THE EIGHTEENTH CENTURY
THE DECORATION OF ENGLISH PORCELAIN
THE CHINA COLLECTOR'S GUIDE
WORCESTER PORCELAIN
BRITISH POTTERY AND PORCELAIN
ENGLISH CERAMICS
ENGLISH WATER-COLOURS
ENGLISH POTTERY AND PORCELAIN MARKS
DICTIONARY OF WATER-COLOUR ARTISTS
(*in preparation*)

Collector's Progress

NEW REVISED EDITION

Stanley W. Fisher

MICHAEL JOSEPH

First published in Great Britain by
MICHAEL JOSEPH
*52 Bedford Square
London, W.C.1*
1957

New revised edition 1971

© 1971 *by Stanley W. Fisher*

All Rights Reserved. No part of this publication may be reproduced, stored in a retrieval system, or transmitted, in any form or by any means, electronic, mechanical, photocopying, recording or otherwise, without the prior permission of the Copyright owner

7181 0941 4

*Printed in Great Britain by
Western Printing Services Ltd, Bristol
and bound by James Burn, Esher*

To
CLARA & MURIEL FISHER
*who in turn have gladly suffered
and encouraged me*

One

When I was small I collected birds' eggs, from which I graduated, as boys do, to stamps. The irresistible urge to collect something is with us at a very early age, earlier in fact than is generally realized, for the tiniest tot amasses a strange variety of toys which he jealously treasures until he casts them all aside in favour of something new. We all know the person who cannot bear to throw anything away, who harbours all kinds of rubbish in the hope that 'it will come in for something one day.' What is he but just another kind of collector?

I suppose it is that same acquisitive instinct that causes every urchin to fill his pockets with toffee-papers, pretty glass marbles, bits of elastic, and pieces of string which makes the collector. It is part of our human make-up. But there is more to it than that. An old proverb says truly that 'What the eye cannot see the heart cannot grieve over.' In other words, the collecting 'bug' really bites when the opportunity to see and to admire comes along. Some fortunate people there have always been who have been brought up among lovely things, and whose elders have encouraged them to understand and love them. Others, observant and beauty-loving by nature, have taken the first step as the result of looking through an antique-shop window. But if these pitfalls have been successfully avoided, even into mature age, there are always the museums and the great houses which in recent years perforce have exposed their mellowed contents to the eyes of every stranger willing to pay his half-crown.

When, in such a place, the craft and art of the centuries are gathered together the discerning cannot fail to wish to own something of the same kind. The attraction lies not only in the intrinsic beauty of the specimens, but in the visualization of the human story behind their manufacture and their use.

The seed once planted, the desire to possess is irresistible, and in this regard the collector is bold indeed if he dares to deny that a considerable part of his enjoyment is inspired by exclusive ownership! Enormous sums have been given for individual specimens of great rarity or outstanding merit, sums which are often so at variance with apparent worth as to provoke scorn or even resentment from the ignorant. Even the collector in a small way has to get used to it.

Values in the world of art depend to a great extent on demand. A single wealthy collector can send prices soaring artificially throughout the world, but woe betide the dealers and his fellow-collectors when for any reason he or his agents cease to frequent the auction rooms. For example, when King Farouk fell from power there was an immediate fall in glass paperweight prices. The wise collector does not broadcast his intention to specialize in some rare kind of *objet d'art*, since to do so will put up prices. Instead, he takes into his confidence some trusty dealer who may then bid on his behalf with less fear of competition.

Not so very long ago a collector was looked upon as a 'crank,' and in fact such he may very easily become. There was once a clock lover who filled his rooms with countless examples of the chiming variety. They were very beautiful, but like Markheim in the story, his friends found it difficult to accustom themselves to the alarming cacophony which greeted the striking of every hour! Another doted on tea-pots of every shape and size, so that his home afforded yet another example of the evils of over-specialization. One can have too much of a good thing.

Whether he be a crank or not, the modern collector is in good and rapidly swelling company. I think the truth is that so many people turn to the acquisition of lovely things as an unconscious protest against the bustle and stress of the machine age. 'Hand made' is a term which can be applied to so few new things. Here and there, in some quiet back street, an old cabinet-maker reproduces the masterpieces of Chippendale, Sheraton, or Hepplewhite with loving, gifted hands. In some peaceful village a potter revives the methods and the mood of the medieval slip-ware makers or the stoneware of the Far East of one thousand years ago. Even the village blacksmith, with no horses to shoe and reluctant, sometimes, to install a petrol pump, turns his skilled hand to the making of wrought-iron gates or fire-baskets. But with such rare exceptions the old days of pride in craftsmanship are gone, the groping, so-called 'contemporary' style fails to satisfy, and we turn with relief to slake our thirst for beauty with the relics of former days.

The late G. Owen Wheeler, surely one of the most knowledgeable of all collectors, had this to say about collecting in difficult times. It was during the early years of the last war. I had asked him whether he thought it unpatriotic to go on collecting when so much money was needed for more urgent needs.

'Go on, my boy!' said he earnestly. 'What you spend won't hurt the Government, and what you buy doesn't compete in labour or materials with war needs—only transfers paper from one pocket to another, and helps some tradesman to keep going.'

He went on to say something else. 'We're not all of us individuals equally at war; and one objective in war is that peace which is the true source of all the arts. Indulgence in the arts in war-time is but a form of sincerity, and of insurance, and of hope, with addicts like you and me.'

Wheeler was speaking in time of war. But do not his words apply with at least equal force in our present time of uneasy peace? Putting on one side the acquisitiveness and the pride of ownership, every true collector, it seems to me, must be a sincere lover of beauty, he must believe that his treasures are a tangible insurance or 'nest-egg' against times of need, and he must dare to hope that the world will never again be mad enough to destroy so much that is fine and worth while.

I suppose that every collector is able to point to some influence in his life, or even to one single incident, which set him going. I cannot say, for myself, that I was brought up among antiques, and certainly I found it difficult to spare an occasional copper to buy stamps from the Approval Sheets which trusting dealers send to schoolboys. How well I remember them! Those colourful sets and single mint specimens, each neatly priced and so arranged in rows that they never looked nearly so fine in our albums! Of course, there was a small commission, and in some mysterious way which is not, alas, applicable to adult business, we each one of us managed to sell to each other, and so to satisfy our craving at very small cost. We even kept a suitably priced stamp to pay for the return postage.

My home as a boy was one of three houses in a row which had been built by my grandfather for his three daughters. Its name, Sydenham Villa, its steel engravings, its bead curtains and venetian blinds, and its uncomfortable mahogany furniture were typically middle-class Edwardian. Here, while I collected stamps, my mother collected Worcester porcelain. Not the rare and valuable early Worcester of the third quarter of the eighteenth century, but the rather wishy-washy 'ivory biscuit' of her day, decorated with flowers, staring highland cattle, and luscious fruit. The same ware is, of course, still popular, though nowadays, and particularly during the last war when the Americans fell in love with it, it is vastly more expensive than it used to be.

In order to fill her cabinet and deck her mantelpieces she took advantage of my father's prowess as an oarsman and billiards player. Every regatta and every knock-out competition at the local workmen's club was the prelude to a new acquisition. Only on rare occasions was a plated tankard or cup replica received grudgingly with questions as to who was to keep it clean. To be fair, I believe the real pride which Worcestershire folk took in their native porcelain was the reason why so many clubs gave pieces of it as prizes. In the days of the Grainger family, before its 1888 amalgamation with the bigger company, the Worcester Rowing Club even had special mugs made, one for each crew member, and each bearing a picture of a regatta scene. Tommy Wyatt of Worcester once took me into his private room where he showed me just such a piece. Dealer or not, it was very clear that he would never part with it!

I really grew to love mother's china and, I think, to understand its faded beauty. It had much in common with the stereotyped, languishing Burne-Jones stained glass windows of the little church where we attended twice every Sunday. This appreciation of at least some kind of art was associated with a talent for drawing and painting which I inherited from her, and which in her case was apparent in the form of painted porcelain plaques and drain-pipes decorated with enormous wild flowers and used as umbrella-stands. At the same time she was far from being a helpless Victorian drawing-room miss, taking indeed a great pride in her household goods. How the old copper warming-pan always shone like the sunset of a winter's evening, and how I used to lie in bed listening to the grinding of chains as my father performed his nightly ritual with the grandfather clock! 'Mind you never part with that clock, Stan. It belonged to your grandmother.'

So it was the china, the warming-pan, the clock, the green glass lustres on the parlour mantelpiece, and the blue-printed Staffordshire dinner-ware which together sowed the seed of my collecting life. I saw that these things were loved, and I accepted the fact as being right and proper.

How intriguing it is, looking back, to realize how circumstances apparently unconnected have governed one's life! My grammar-school headmaster was not only one of the wisest of men but also an artist who could teach his craft and inspire a love for it. He it was who taught me to appreciate beauty of form and significance of line, the proper recognition of which is so necessary for full understanding of true craftsmanship.

When I was seventeen, in 1922, I was sent to a training college for teachers. Like so many youths I had not the faintest idea of what I would like to do with my life. Part of my training took the form of 'school practice' in various local schools, one of which was actually part of the college, and built within its walls. Thither one summer morning, some half-dozen of us went, full of enthusiasm and entirely lacking in skill, to be sent to the various classrooms. For myself, my hesitant progress up a steep, dimly-lit stone staircase was the way, had I known it, to what was to be my absorbing interest in after life.

I knocked upon the door at the top of the stairway, opened it, and entered a large classroom in which some sixty boys were seated. There was complete silence, but as I crossed the floor each lad raised his eyes appraisingly for a moment, looked from me to the teacher at his desk and set straightway to his work again. Here, at least, was a most strange thing! In my previous limited experience the entrance of a student was the welcome signal for a rising crescendo of whispering, banging of lockers, and clatter of hobnailed boots!

The master stood up, shook me by the hand, and introduced himself. 'I'm Tipping,' said he. 'Sit down and tell me about yourself.'

He drew up a chair beside his own tall one, and we sat down.

I find it difficult to recall my first impressions of the man who was to have such an influence on my life. I think, perhaps, it was one of kindly gentleness and understanding. Features very like those of the late Earl Baldwin of Bewdley (Stanley Baldwin, as we called him in Worcestershire), austere, with deep-set eyes below bushy eyebrows, a deep, clean-shaven upper lip, ruddy complexion, and thinning tow-coloured hair. A shrewd, stern face which could yet in an instant light up puckishly with a humorous lift of the eyebrows and a pursing of the lips.

Conrad Tipping was of Herefordshire yeoman stock. One could more easily picture him behind a plough than before a blackboard, with his stocky body, sturdy legs, and powerful hands. Yet it was clear that his reputation as a schoolmaster was well-deserved, if only for that perfect discipline of which I had early proof. Kind he certainly was, and wise in the ways of boys and of his fellow-men, but never did he allow the common touch to degenerate into familiarity.

'Keep yourself on a pedestal, my boy!' was his advice to me. And good advice it was, though I have often suspected that his apparent aloofness may in the beginning have been a cover for his complete deafness, a legacy of his student days.

I heard more about Tipping from the senior students. He was a B.A. of London and a Fellow of the Royal Historical Society. He was, moreover, a part-time lecturer in Advanced English Literature in the college itself. But as far as I was concerned, a significant fact was that his wife owned a hotel in the town.

What has all this to do with collecting? I can hear the question, and it is best to skip the uneventful years of teaching during which I had no thought of ever taking an interest in antiques of any kind. Then came the autumn of 1932, the offer of a country headship and of a school house, and a marriage hastily planned for a few days after Christmas Day.

Where should we go for our honeymoon at such a time of the year? That was a poser, and I am certain that some inner guidance prompted the answer—why not go to Mrs. Tipping's hotel? So it was agreed.

I wrote to my old tutor, for the first time since leaving college. Could my wife and I spend a week's holiday (not a honeymoon, you will note!) at his wife's hotel?

His answer came by return. He remembered me, and yes, it would be quite all right.

So, late in the afternoon of the 29th, we reached the hotel. A maid took us through the hall and down a long passage to a small room at the far end of which was a glass-panelled door, at which she knocked, very loudly.

'Come in!' called a familiar voice.

We entered, and the maid left us. Tipping rose from a chair behind his desk, and met me with outstretched hand. Then . . .

'When was the wedding?' he asked.

Introductions completed, we sat down together to talk. I forget what was said, but we were delighted when he invited us to use his study as our own. He himself, it was explained, would be out during the daytime, but he would be glad to chat with us in the evenings, after dinner, if we had nothing better to do.

During the following week I grew to know every inch of that cosy little room. It was a wooden extension built on to the back of the house. Two gaily curtained windows and a french window caught the morning sun, and overlooked a pleasant little stone-flagged, walled courtyard. The opposite wall was lined with bookshelves, and in the centre of the room was a large rectangular Cromwellian table. Beneath each window was a low set of shelves, and the end wall opposite the door was filled by a corner fireplace, a small chest-upon-chest, and a roll-top desk, before which stood

Tipping's own high leather-covered arm-chair. Another lower chair, deep and comfortable, was placed before the fire, and the only other piece of furniture, if such it could be called, was an enormous mortar of golden-brown elm-wood which stood beside the french window.

For some days, as was very natural, we were interested more in each other than in our surroundings, but as the week drew to a close we began to pay more and more attention to the contents of the room. We idly turned over the pages of some of the books, and inevitably our eyes were drawn to the plates, bowls, jugs, and other bric-à-brac which crowded the book-case tops, and to the pictures and other objects which hung upon the walls. They were nice to admire, though we knew little enough about them.

Con (for so we thought of him, though not daring so to address him) saw our interest, and without trying to press his own evident enthusiasm upon us he brought a piece here and a piece there into the conversation. Upon the deep triangular mantelpiece stood a tall figure, perhaps two feet or more in height, of a girl in classic style, gracefully balancing a pitcher upon one bare shoulder. A Minton piece, he explained, most beautifully modelled and sparingly gilded. We agreed it was very lovely, but he smiled and showed us instead, upon the chest in the corner, a bottle-shaped vase in glowing turquoise-blue, and as we passed our hands gingerly over its glistening surface he talked of the fine colour and perfect glaze which mark the best Chinese monochromes.

When we had gazed our fill, on to the figure of a Chinese beggar, ugly but infinitely wise, carved from a gnarled, misshapen root of some iron-hard wood, and to an elephant intricately inlaid with exquisite enamels of blue and green. And all the time the pieces seemed to come to life under his description, and the craftsmen who had fashioned them so many years ago. But from time to time, with a sudden change of mood and a merry twinkle in his eye, he told us graphically of the argument and the haggling which had preceded each lucky 'buy.'

I remember there were many other fine pieces to be examined and admired. An old truncheon emblazoned, as the fashion once was, with a coat-of-arms in brilliant colours and gold, a Tibetan prayer-wheel of brass, a carved head of a saint from some old church, an inlaid tile from nearby Hales Abbey, bearing the arms of Aragon and Castile, a framed piece of Stuart 'stump-work' embroidery, a large round plaque modelled by Émile Lessore at Mintons, and a great coat-of-arms in 'curled-paper work,' its once gay colours mellowed by the years. All these treasures hung upon the walls, but in a corner, to itself, hung a more modern and intimate thing, a framed newspaper cutting and a picture of an old lady threading an impossible number of cottons through the eye of a small needle. It was his mother, then well over eighty, he said.

Our interest now fully roused, he bade us sit with him around the fire, for it was a cold night. He opened the top cupboard of the chest and produced a bottle of his favourite cherry-brandy and three wide-footed cordial glasses. There we sat at our ease, and watched as he then opened one by one the drawers of the lower part of the same chest, taking out piece after piece of pottery or porcelain for our examination and for his own description. He was teaching us now, deliberately and with all the trained skill at his command, but this same ritual was one in which I was to take a fuller part on countless occasions in later years, an exciting, absorbing exchange of opinion, deduction, and argument which ended to our mutual satisfaction in an attribution to which we both agreed.

On this first essay we were content to listen and to absorb, to handle reverently each piece of early ware, and to examine under his instruction the dainty flower-painting, the tiny landscapes, or the exotic Chinese figures upon it. He told us that they were the results of his previous week's search in the town's many antique and junk shops, not yet finally identified, many of them 'puzzles,' and only some few of them to be added to his permanent collection.

By this time I, at any rate, was eager to see more of this kind of china, so very different from my mother's collection, and I was only too pleased when he suggested we might go to see his cabinets in the public drawing-room on the first floor. He went ahead, 'to see if the coast is clear,' and I noticed above the doorway a clear rubbing of the well-known caution to grave-despoilers which guards Shakespeare's Stratford tomb.

He beckoned us in, and carefully unlocked each of the four cabinets which stood against the walls, throwing wide open their glazed doors. The impact of so much colour was breathtaking, and for a moment we stood and looked helplessly at the crowded shelves. For crowded they were! Hopelessly, bewilderingly crowded, with no attempt at classification or colour-scheme. Dear old Con and his cabinet arrangement! What headaches it caused him before he was harried into taking action! But that is to anticipate, and we were content, then, to wonder at whatever we might be shown.

Bowl upon upturned bowl, cream-jugs inside wide, handleless tea-cups, figures, tea-pots, and sauceboats, all ranked and piled, tight-packed, against the background of plates and saucers which leaned against the cabinet backs. Worcester and Lowestoft porcelain jostled with Whieldon and Ralph Wood figures, and delicate Chinese *famille-rose* lived perforce on friendly terms with the iridescent glass of Roman England. Only one cabinet, in a corner by itself, offered a plainer, uncrowded face, for in it was nothing but ware decorated in the palest blue. I was so attracted that I walked across for a closer view.

It was clear that many pieces bore decoration which even to my unskilled eye had an Oriental appearance, though to be sure, I thought, the Chinese mandarins and ladies were surely abnormally tall and willowy! And where were their typical slanting almond eyes? I bent down to look even more closely, and Con and my wife walked over to join me.

'Surely this is Chinese porcelain?' I asked, seeking to air a little of my newly acquired knowledge.

Con smiled, and gently disillusioned me. He went on to talk of the first early attempts to imitate Chinese porcelain in this country, of the painstaking copying of the alien ware, even to the marks, and of the difference between 'hard' and 'soft' paste. I learnt for the first time about underglaze cobalt blue, of transfer-printing, and of the Dutch *lange lisẓen* (or 'slender maidens') which the rough English translated into the cruder though descriptive 'long elizas.' He spoke in metaphors of the rustic maiden in her sprigged muslin dress, the poor relation of her brocaded cousin, and of how they could never live together, but must always be housed far apart. And as he talked, and the winter gale outside howled along the quiet street, a love for this simpler, restrained ware grew within me, and in that moment I think I resolved to make a collection of it one day.

At length, long after the house was still, we left our friend and went up to our own room on a higher floor. My mind was awhirl as I tried in vain to set into some kind of order all the information which had been given.

In vain. I was only quite determined that I, too, must collect without delay, and my last conscious thought was concerned with what I imagined might be a good way to setting about it!

It was to be expected that during the few days which remained to us my wife and I re-examined much that we had been shown, for Con had done us the honour of trusting us with his keys. He had also showed us, before he left the house after breakfast the following morning, where he kept his books on collecting, and I lost no time in learning as much as I could. To very little purpose, it must be admitted, but then I was so very enthusiastic!

In those early days my wife was not so wildly enthusiastic. She was content and happy to see me so absorbed, but she was not bitten by the collecting bug. She was wise enough, I think, to foresee the perpetual penury which only a collector knows, and she decided that two such in one family could spell nothing but early acquaintance with the workhouse! On the other hand, it is true to say that she has never discouraged me, not even when for the first time I paid such an enormous sum as £60 for a single piece of latish Worcester porcelain! Indeed, as she handled my 'finds' and learned more about them her interest grew—especially when, as sometimes happened, I sold a duplicate at a profit. A man has much to be thankful for.

When Tipping joined us on our last evening I tremblingly made the suggestion which had been in my mind for several days. Would he, could he possibly bear to sell me some of the pieces he might not want?

His reply came without hesitation. Certainly he would, and happy to do it. What is more, I could take them at the silly prices he had paid, and I might take my time in paying for them!

So it was arranged, and when we left the next day we took with us into Worcestershire a large cardboard box full of pottery and porcelain. Small pieces, all of them, but every one of interest, all perfect and typical of their kind, and none costing more than a few shillings.

No sooner were we at home than we sent him a piece of our wedding cake, and before me as I write is his letter of thanks.

'Thank you, cordially, for your wedding cake and for your letter. If wishes count (and I'm sure they do) you are in for a ripe old age, both of you, and "roses all the way."

'I'm glad you had my "bits"; they are one's children, in a way. I shall have several other things for you and shall wish to make you a present of them, for I've no note of the prices, or else they were gifts.

'I reply rather breathlessly—I have a vague "few minutes" before a call to supper and then I'm to go up to the hills for some fresh air.

'I haven't found the Nankin plate for you yet, though I don't doubt I shall do so. About six dealers are looking out. I want a well-potted one with a good border and a typical Chinese sketch within. I have a bulb bowl in Nankin ware, blue and white, heavy, I'll hand over if I fail in the plate quest.'

As a matter of fact a plate was found, though that did not prevent his giving me the bowl also, a hexagonal one painted with breaking waves. These pieces joined those which formed my first collection, which was proudly displayed on two shelves fixed for that purpose along one wall of our tiny dining-room.

The exposed pieces quickly accumulated a thick layer of dust, and I was obliged to start a practice I have followed ever since. A collector who allows others to wash and dust his treasures has only himself to blame when something gets broken.

That is how my first collection began. I can even remember many of the pieces. A Staffordshire cider-mug painted with flowers in gay enamels, the Nankin plate and bowl, a Worcester Queen Victoria Jubilee plate, printed in red, a Meissen cup and saucer painted with flowers in puce enamel, bearing the crossed swords mark, two Ridgway cane-ware 'Gothic' jugs, one putty-coloured and one buff, a bottle vase of old *millefiori* glass, brilliant as a rainbow, a little lustre jug by Allertons, and a Chinese brush-bowl in grey monochrome, finely crackled. The pride of all was a Japanese breakfast set of the thinnest egg-shell porcelain, painted with microscopic flowers, birds, and tiger-hunts, beside which lay a magnifying glass for the benefit of admiring friends.

It may be thought remarkable that I should have such a clear recollection of these first pieces after more than twenty years, especially as all have found other and, I hope, equally appreciative owners.

After all, is it not very natural? They were, in truth, my 'children,' and the arrival of a larger family during the years between has in no way diminished either my memory of or my affection for them.

Two

WHEN all is said and done there is no royal road to collecting, to the knowledge of pastes and patterns, shapes and glazes, but persistent attention, interest, and above all, handling. Prices come the same way. I say to myself, 'This is worth so and so to me,' and I am for ever comparing the prices asked for the same kind of goods in different shops.

The same applies, of course, whether one collects furniture, silver, pictures, or any other sort of antiques. One's original choice on what to collect depends on personal taste, on the depth of one's pocket, or, as in my own case, upon the way in which one is led to begin. But one great advantage the china collector has over most of his fellows—he can house his pieces in a tiny home, and at the same time beautify it. Moreover there is such a wide variety of wares from which to choose, and a range of prices to suit every purse.

When I was telling how my appetite was first whetted I did not explain how it was that my teacher, though stone deaf, was yet able to take part in our conversations and to chaffer, as one must, with dealers.

It is an interesting story, because it illustrates how collecting can transform a man's whole life and character.

His disability made Con a recluse. He shunned every kind of company, shutting himself away in his study with his books, or else tramping alone for hours on his beloved hills.

Then one day Captain G. Owen Wheeler came to stay in the hotel, unknown, rather eccentric in his habits, but very wise in the ways of men.

He quickly summed up the situation, and by sheer persistence, ignoring a desire to be left alone that was all too plainly expressed, he became a frequent evening visitor to the little room.

The two men played innumerable games of chess, which both loved, until one evening Wheeler took in, as if by chance, several pieces which he had that day acquired from local shops.

The result was just as he had expected.

Tipping admired, examined, inquired, and with such a teacher he learnt very quickly. He came out of his shell, a changed man. Deafness had not mattered very much until now, once he had resolved to accept loneliness as his lot, but with the new interest came the desire and the need to meet others who shared his new enthusiasm. His first bulky hearing aid was inefficient, but it sufficed. Then, several years after I became a collector, he bought a new, expensive model, and I happened to be staying with him at the time.

I breakfasted alone, and when I entered his study he was standing in the open french window. Now, since he was half-turned away from me I fully expected to have to walk right up to him and touch his arm in order to reveal my presence. Not a bit of it! As I closed the door behind me, so he turned to face me, a glad smile on his face.

'Stan,' said he quietly, 'just before you came in I heard the birds sing for the first time in thirty years. Thank God for science.'

When we were together he always removed the tiring headband, and when I wanted to speak I would give him a nudge. He never admitted it, but I am sure he found that deafness was a remarkable aid to a poker face when bargaining with a dealer!

'How much do you want for this?' (the hearing aid tucked away out of sight in a waistcoat pocket).

'Five pounds.'

Silence, and a deliberate examination of some other piece.

'Well, say four pounds.'

More silence, but a watchful eye on the dealer's reactions.

'Call it three, then, and that's the best I can do!'

The critical moment had arrived, and the aid was carefully adjusted.

'What did you say?'

'Three pounds!' Loudly. And the deal was done!

Owen Wheeler was but one of the many delightful people I have met in the search for antiques—why is it that nearly all those who love 'old Beautiful,' as Rohan calls it, are such delightful people?—but I have never met anyone so knowledgeable or more respected 'in the trade.' A bank manager at twenty-one, a professional soldier for many years and, following a short but intensive study of furniture, metalwork, and china in later life, a man recognized thereafter as being an authority second to none. He was so prominent that he was chosen as manager of the early Antique Dealers' Fairs organized by the B.A.D.A., the final judge (from whose decision there was no appeal) of the 'rightness' of every piece displayed on the many stands.

A tall man, with a chest like a barrel, and a presence compelling attention in any company. Autocratic, self-opinionated perhaps, but ever genial, generous to a fault, and kindness itself. He dressed always in ratcatcher, and favoured spotted bow ties. 'Fine old English gentleman' is perhaps a hackneyed phrase, but I cannot find a better.

I know now how fortunate I was to have two such teachers. Both were my elders by many years, but they took me into a comradeship which led my feet along so many pleasant paths, and which was the 'open sesame' to many a dealer's confidence. Even now, when I sometimes ask, 'Did you ever know Owen Wheeler?' I am welcomed for his sake. Not so often, sadly enough, these last few years. There is all the world of difference between the Frank Partridges of the antique world, who loved their pieces and were sad to see them go, and those who in recent years think only of monetary values.

By their manners and lack of real knowledge shall ye know them!

So, in my early collecting years between 1932 and the outbreak of war, 'The Three Musketeers,' as Owen called us, hunted together.

I use the word 'hunted' advisedly. Not that we were often able to get into my car together and set out for the day. Con and I did this often, but Wheeler's movements were always as erratic and uncertain as the man himself, and having no settled home he never stayed for long in one place. A threesome was therefore a rare and long-anticipated red-letter day, and the months between were spanned by long letters full of collecting gossip.

With Tipping and me antique hunting had to take second place to teaching, but with our friend it was a profession. For years he had scoured the countryside the happy possessor of the open cheque of a world-famous dealer. Now, having found the courage to forsake what seems to me to have been a collector's seventh heaven, he found pieces for himself.

For himself, did I say? Rather, for his friends!

The truth is that Wheeler had ideas of house furnishing which would have driven any woman to distraction. They were for the most part sound, to be sure, but no housewife could fail to be discouraged to find, on returning from a holiday, that the entire contents of her drawing-room had been replaced by new acquisitions! So it was that he was to be found in Cheltenham one month, in Ipswich the next, then in Penrith, and so on throughout the year. And the house of each friend with whom he tarried was filled with his finds, while at the same time the overflow was dispatched by post and rail to anyone who was willing to give houseroom. Ipswich Museum was amongst the many which rejoiced in loan collections of his furniture, treen, and pictures.

It is always good for a collector to have one notable piece which sets his standard. Mine was a noble 10-inch Chinese 'tea-dust' bowl, mounted on a teak stand, cunningly pieced together and carved with emblematic peaches of longevity. The story is that the tea-dust glaze was reserved for the Emperor, and mine had the impressed seal-mark of the Yung-Cheng (1723–35) period. A rather dull piece at first sight, brownish-green in colour and flecked with greenish gold. It came to life only when a ray of sunlight slanted across its dimpled surface.

This lovely bowl was well to the fore on the Moss stand at the 1938 Fair at Grosvenor House. It was the 'show piece,' and as such Wheeler recognized it when he gave the stands his final 'vetting' on the eve of the opening.

'That's mine!' he said.

The show was to be opened by Queen Mary. Poking inquisitively here and there with her umbrella, she made the round of the treasures upon the stands. Her escort, Wheeler himself, stood a pace behind, at her elbow.

Inevitably, she paused to look at the bowl, and inevitably she fell in love with it. Was it for sale?

There was an embarrassing pause.

Moss cast a despairing glance at the imperturbable Wheeler, who thereupon uttered the terrible words:

'I'm sorry, Ma'am, but that piece is not for sale!'

Collecting, you see, knows no law. Not even that of lese-majesty.

A week later it came to me with the usual request, and Wheeler left it to me in his will.

Another fine piece arrived at the same time from Hancock, the famous dealer in Chinese porcelain. The postman delivered a large cardboard box. Inside the lid was a complimentary note, another request, but this time at second-hand. Layer upon layer of tissue-paper, and at last a large cylindrical bowl of the finest Nankin, the true sapphire blue which has the clarity of the sky after rain, cunningly painted with tall mandarins. The removal of still more packing, and I came at last upon the knobbed cover wherein lay the main interest of the piece. It was not Chinese, but Dutch delft, a clever imitation which some previous owner had caused to be made.

This particular bowl did not stay with me very long. (One of the penalties of this kind of guardianship was that one never quite knew when the command would come to send the goods elsewhere!) But while I had it I was always reminded of the human side of collecting. How was the original cover broken? How many other hands than mine had caressed the cool, smooth glaze, and what other eyes had peered into its impossible perspective?

It is amusing and often fascinating to remember through how many different eras even an eighteenth-century piece has lived. One pictures the silks and satins, and the knee-breeches, the powdered wigs, and whole paraphernalia of gracious living it has seen.

We are so accustomed to seeing our treasures in a modern setting that we tend to forget how alien they are to it.

Here is an example of what I mean.

During one of my many visits to Stoke, I was delighting in the Spode Works Museum. Cabinet after cabinet, deep-set into the walls of a lofty, oak-lined hall, each filled with pieces that sparkled and glowed under the fierce glare of fluorescent lamps.

Then, without a word, Mr. Gresham Copeland pressed a switch, and the glare gave place to the soft light of a few candle-power.

What a transformation!

Violet-blues lost their crudity, harsh greens softened to the colour of a close-mown English lawn, and life came to drabs and browns in undertones which had not been there an instant before.

'You see, we often forget that they were meant to be seen by candlelight,' said Mr. Copeland.

My appetite whetted by Wheeler's pieces, I threw myself whole-heartedly into the collecting game. Every letter from him or from Tipping was a vicarious adventure into a new, fascinating world. And every antique shop held the promise of some remarkable 'find,' which in my imagination lay tucked away in some dusty corner until I should recognize it for what it was, and pick it up, of course, at some silly price.

The association of ideas is a curious thing, and surely responsible for some of our happiest memories.

With me, at any rate, a piece of bric-à-brac recalls vividly to mind the whole circumstance of its finding.

Sometimes the picture is one of a quiet Cotswold village golden under a summer sun, of the monotonous dirge of a distant tractor echoing across the rounded wolds, of wheeling aircraft in a fleecy sky, and of a picnic lunch eaten in the shelter of a mossy wall. A polished tea-caddy of Tonbridge ware, with its cross-sectioned picture of Nottingham Castle, reminds me of narrow Friar Street and of William Pease, whom I first met after an early breakfast at a commercial hotel along the London Road, Derby. He is only one of the many dealers each one of whom is associated with one particular piece or some outstanding adventure.

What a horrible word it is! Dealers! It savours over-much of the second-hand shop and 'the ring.' But can you find a better? 'Fine art dealer' will do, perhaps, but it is a term so often belied both by the man and his wares.

Whatever he may call himself, his friendship and help are essential. Without them the collector must have the hide of an elephant and a face of brass if he is to pay visit after visit, looking around and rarely buying anything because what he seeks is like the jam, always tomorrow.

For the first few years I did not dare to venture into the specialists' shops, at least when I was alone. Not that it mattered, for until I set about buying 'blue and white' in earnest anything was grist that came into my mill. So gradually I met dealers up and down the country, always asking questions, and learning all the time.

Much that I was told was wrong. A general dealer cannot be expected to know a great deal about everyone of the many kinds of antique which he must stock, and his aim is rather to teach himself to recognize quality and expert craftsmanship in whatever guise.

'I do not know what it is, but I do know that it is good.'

One day I set out early to visit a little Cotswold town which cuts a straight line up a breakneck hill. I had never been there before, and immediately opposite the spot where I parked my car was a double bow-windowed shop, newly-painted, with the word 'Antiques' over the door.

The rather dim interior was hidden by several large chests-of-drawers which formed the background of the window display, and I entered to find a young fellow of rather frail appearance standing in his shirt-sleeves behind a wash-tub.

He greeted me in a most cultured voice, and since it was clear that his chores, whatever they were, could not wait upon my pleasure, I offered to give him a helping hand. He accepted gratefully, and explained that he was washing china. He was clearly new to the game, for when I pointed out that a tulip-shaped vase in his hand was early Chelsea, he almost dropped it!

Apparently his mother had 'set him up.' He knew nothing about antiques (though he loved them), but hoped to learn.

If I had been unscrupulous I could have picked up more bargains than I could have carried home. I carried on a long argument with myself all the way home as to why I had not done so. As it was, and because the little I knew I placed at his disposal, we became friends. He has prospered, though because he is a Quaker, and in spite of his frailty drove an ambulance during the war, his business suffered a temporary setback during those hateful years. His four showrooms are crowded with lovely things (properly priced nowadays!) and his assistants wisely refrain from badgering his customers. His prices are marked in plain figures, which is wise because the use of a code is embarrassing if one wishes to know the price of a great many pieces.

A cipher has its uses, of course, but it does enable the unscrupulous dealer to adjust his prices according to the appearances of his customers! On the other hand, one may well rejoice when a dealer makes one free of its inner meaning, not only as regards selling price, but cost price also.

When a dealer sets up in a small community he is usually happy to welcome the inevitable competitor. One may well hesitate to make a special journey to visit one shop, whereas two or three cannot fail to tempt. One of those who had opened up next door to Roger, as we will call him, had the seeing eye. I was attracted not only by a good window display and a well-kept little shop inside, but also by a notice which invited the public to inspect 'The Crypt.'

I went in.

'May I look round, please?' and the lady assistant smilingly stepped aside as I descended a short, steep stair, turned a sharp corner at the bottom, and without any warning stepped straight into Ali Baba's cave!

Picture a perfect little chapel of golden Cotswold stone, its vaulted roof supported by a single, central column. Small pieces of furniture, all of good quality and lovingly polished, standing here and there upon faded Persian rugs partially hiding the unevenly flagged floor. China, silver, ormolu, and glass flashing and sparkling under chandeliers whose mellow light completes the illusion of a miniature fairyland.

Collecting does indeed lead into beautiful places, whether natural or man-made. That is a part of its fascination. Here was a 'dealer,' a Cambridge graduate withal, who had come upon a coal-cellar and transformed it into a treasure cave. Here, he showed me, cut deeply into the central column, were the grooved rope-marks made by the former tenant, a vandal if ever there was one! But he could not explain to me why such a medieval gem was to be found under a quite commonplace cottage in a village street.

I soon discovered that a friendly dealer loves nothing better than an argument. He is not averse, even, to a mild form of haggling, especially if he be on the buying side of the deal!

Whenever I take down my copy of *Worcester Porcelain*, by R. L. Hobson, I remember every word of a conversation which was prompted by its purchase.

I was staying in Cheltenham at the time, and one evening I went out to offer to lend my new book to a dealer. I took also a bowl nicely painted with flowers, and an unusual Worcester teapot with the crossed-swords mark, put on, like the decoration, in imitation of Meissen. I knew he would be interested, because he set himself up with some justification as an expert.

We got straight to business.

'How much do you want for this?' (the Hobson).

'It's to lend you, if you'd like it.'

'Won't you sell it?'

'No!'

'What did you give for it?'

'Sixty-three bob and two shillings postage.'

'Sure you won't sell?'

'Yes, quite sure.'

A grunt, and over passed the bowl.

'That's Chamberlain's! Where did you get it?'

'Privately' (the stock answer!), 'and I think it may be Wall. See, it's pictured in Hobson!'

'Gound base, careful work, pattern number. It's Chamberlain's. Can I buy it?'

'I don't want to sell it.'

'I'd like it. Would you take a quid for it?'

'No,' I said.

'Well, twenty-five bob?'

'All right.'

'Can you find me any more?'

'I'll see,' said I, knowing just where to lay my hands on a part service.

Then came the turn of the tea-pot. On with the spectacles, out with the lens, and on with a stronger light.

'German,' says he, loudly.

'Think so?' (as carelessly as possible).

More looking.

'H'm! Chalky base. Worcester colour but Lowestoft china!'

'You think so?' said I, again.

'I don't like it. I don't think it's Worcester.'

'So you said.'

'D'YE WANT TO SELL IT?' (almost shouted).

'NO!' said I, as loudly.

'Well, I'd like to show it to a couple of friends of mine.'

'Show it to them by all means,' I replied.

Out came Binn's *Worcester Marks*, and a search was made, with much puffing and blowing.

Triumphantly, 'See, it isn't recorded!'

'That's why I prize it!'

More fingering, and lens work, and stroking.

'Can't I make you an offer for it?'

'No.'

'What price d'ye put on it?'

'None, but I know it's Worcester, unique, and a desirable piece.'

'Sure you won't sell?'

'Yes, but as a matter of curiosity, tell me what it's worth.'

'Would three pounds tempt you?' he said after a bit.

'Damnation, NO!'

'A fiver?'
'I wouldn't look at it.'
'I bet you paid five bob for it,' he said.
'You're dead right!'
'Well, come on! Sell it!'
'No,' said I, 'YOU wouldn't if you'd found it!'
'No,' he confessed. 'I wouldn't. Let me keep it for a bit and I'll show it to my clients. It's a most interesting piece of old Worcester.'
'Old Worcester, is it?'
'Right!' says he, wryly.
'You'd like to know Owen Wheeler agrees with you.

Well, I knew my tea-pot was worth at least £20, and since money was nothing to his clients, and a great deal to me, he eventually got his wish!

The same dealer also liked Sheffield Plate, and one Saturday morning I took along a most unusual decanter stand. Ordinary coasters are common enough, but this one was double, and on wheels, and I knew he would be interested. I had picked it up in a dirty little junk-shop for 5s. It was so filthy that it scarcely looked even worth that much, but a little whiting and meths worked wonders.

Sure enough, as soon as he saw it he grew excited, I could see.

A lot of roundabout talk. Hedging. Coyness.

At last, 'I wouldn't mind doing a swap, just to do you a good turn,' I said.

'Here's a little Worcester jug, blue and white.'

No, I wanted colour!

'Well, will you give me ten bob, and you can have this "Chinese" Worcester one?'

'No money,' said I, and toyed absently with an early, silvershape Chelsea one. It was coloured, and a really lovely thing.

He gulped and made an effort.

'All right! I've got it marked three pun ten,' he complained.

'Foolish!' said I.

'Here's my list. I gave two fifteen for it!'

So I had my jug and he had his Sheffield Plate, and we were both satisfied.

Dealers soon get to know when a collector is 'in the market' for a particular kind of goods, and the telephone is a mixed blessing when one is short of ready money!

Mine rang one evening, and a dealer who lived in our nearest town told me he had a few pieces he thought I'd like, early Wall Worcester, with Chinese figures in colours.

When I got there he had the pieces laid out on a table.

I appraised the tea-bowl and saucer, the large bread-and-butter plate, and the bowl. All perfect, all sweet and lovely—and kept my mouth tightly shut.

I knew him!

I made the mental reservation that I might run to £9.

We sat by the fire and smoked, and talked about the 'flu and the weather, and old deals, and all the time he kept hedging towards the pieces and ever I hedged away.

At last he got desperate, and said, 'Well, you don't care for them, then?'

'I didn't say so. What are you asking for the lot?'

'Four pounds ten,' says he.

'Is that the best you can do?' I asked, to hide my relief.

'It is,' he said.

'I'll have 'em.'

That was my best buy since I had begun collecting. The bowl was the early Redcliff Backs ('Lowdin's') edition, with the 'long elizas'' faces washed in red, not pencilled or transfer-outlined in black, as the later Wall pieces are. The bowl and saucer were the same, and the big plate had the black outline.

One of the first dealers I met was a little ex-valet named Charlie Mitchell, who had a tiny shop in Winchcombe Street, Cheltenham. Everyone loved him, a gentle, kindly old man, who seemed to care little whether he sold or not, and who always welcomed a chat. He was knowledgeable, yet never pressed his opinion, and I never heard him say a bad word about anyone. His best pieces he kept tucked away in a poky little room behind the shop, where a fire burned winter and summer, and a tea-pot stewed all day long on the rusty hob. That was his holy of holies, and only his particular friends were invited into it.

The first purchase I made from him was a part service of early Worcester, some dozen pieces, all carefully painted in puce with delicate flower-sprays, and finely gilded. This was in 1936, and I remember that his price was £5.

It happened that I was in Cheltenham at the time of a big two-day sale in Gloucester. He showed me the catalogue, which among other things listed a few blue and white leaf dishes which I thought I might like. At first Charlie said he wouldn't go, but at last he consented to attend the first day. He did, and reported nothing interesting but a wooden or nut 'hedgehog' with a brass snout!

'I shan't trouble to go for THAT!' he said, and we left it at that, though knowing Charlie I had my doubts.

Sure enough, the sale was on the Thursday and Friday, and on Saturday morning, about ten-thirty, I found him in his shop dressed in morning suit, as smart as you please.

'Where's the wedding, Charlie?' I asked.

'I've just this minute got back from Gloucester to pick up my things,' and the old rascal produced the nut ornament, probably coconut, which turned out to be not a hedgehog but a porcupine with his back drilled for tooth-picks. French or Dutch, we decided.

'How much?' I asked.

'Fifty bob,' he replied.

'No,' I said firmly. 'Got any pottery?'

'No,' in turn, then:

'Lord, I forgot! What d'ye think of this?' and he took from a cupboard a figure of a bull (very, very male!) in flowing, mingled Whieldon glazes, browns and gold. It was massively legged, and stood on a green, oval base which was hollow.

Instantly I thought to myself—Whieldon influence, 1750 onwards. Moreover, it had a dog whistle at the front end of the base, and the back was pierced for—yes! Tooth-picks!

I asked him as innocently as I could where it was made. He said he thought it might be foreign, and though he liked the glazes he could not place the yellowish clay.

Cautiously I edged round to the price.

TWENTY-FIVE SHILLINGS!

I left with the bull, but within half an hour I had parted with it to another collecting friend in exchange for a Bristol glass barrel-shaped mug with trailed decoration, and a museum piece in the shape of a frail wine-glass made by exiled Venetian workmen at Newent, Gloucestershire, in the late eighteenth century.

It is a bad mistake to show one's finds to someone you like to please. He sparkled, and bubbled about my lovely bull, raved and purred so piteously that I hadn't the heart to refuse him. I firmly believe I could have had anything in his whole collection! At any rate, a letter arrived the morning following my return home.

'I spent a sleepless night due to the incessant bellowing of six maddened pottery cows—two blue and white, two black, and the milk-jug by me! They were all craving motherhood. The arrival of a stately bull, God sent, made their hearts beat wildly—any offspring they have you can have your pick of! M—— has just been in, fell headlong and gasped for a full minute. I said nary a word. He said, "First ever seen, should be in the British Museum. Sure it was made by Whieldon 1730–40" (IT WASN'T) "for they used a different glaze from Staffordshire!" It's the most interesting thing in my collection, and NEVER for sale.'

Few people knew Charlie's private troubles. His wife was incurably insane, though harmless, and he would not let her be put away. Twice every day this gentle, fastidious man bathed her. He did all the shopping, and prepared all the meals. He fed her like a baby, and put her to bed. And with all this he was never anything but cheerful.

Only once did I see him close to tears, when he related how on his arrival home the evening before she had told him with pride that she had made a pudding for his evening meal. So she had, but it was made with washing-powder.

The last war was in its final stages when his wife died suddenly in her sleep. At last, we all thought, Charlie will have the peace and quiet he has long deserved.

It was not to be.

A fortnight later, as he was returning home from his shopping one Saturday morning, an American lorry swept quickly round a blind corner.

Charlie jumped for his life, but he was not so agile as he used to be.

Three

IT is rumoured that a very well-known collector and authority once gave lessons in collecting at so much an hour. This may or may not be true, but it is certainly a fact that dealers have been known to advertise to the effect that they were prepared to buy pottery by the pound! As some of the rarest and most valuable pottery is also the lightest—Ralph Wood 'Tobies' for instance—the idea is commendable, though I have not heard that anything ever came of it.

Dealers are fortunate because so many things are brought to them for sale, and most of them welcome the shabby, down-at-heel folk who hesitate on the doorstep before proffering a brown-paper parcel or a covered shopping basket.

But not all!

I was in a well-known dealer's shop one day when a little old lady who had clearly seen better days produced from her purse an old coin. It may have been silver or even gold, but the dealer stayed not to inquire.

'Madam,' he shouted, 'I am here to sell and not to buy! Will you please get out of my shop?'

I am glad to know that the biter was badly bitten shortly afterwards when a wealthy nobleman noted for his untidiness of dress was greeted in the same cavalier manner. He, at least, had come to buy, and to buy well, but he did not stay to say so.

Pieces have often been brought to me for an opinion, but they are unfortunately seldom for sale. If they are, and if they are of any interest, I cannot help giving an unbiased opinion (cursing myself later for doing so), and once again they pass hopelessly out of my reach. How I wish I were a doctor!

'Oh, yes, a pretty little piece, isn't it? A present from a grateful patient, you know!'

I had not been collecting for very long when in sheer desperation I decided to advertise. The first reply was from a lady who had a box of fourteen Staffordshire figures for sale; not the early kind, but enormous Victorian mantelpiece ornaments, including Dick Turpin, Red Riding Hood, Hamlet, Louis Napoleon, and so on. She asked £25 for the lot. I demurred. Well, she'd take £20 if I thought it too much. I refused to have any truck at all.

A few days afterwards I told a friend about them, and he went to try his luck. He made a little more progress, for he got her down to £15.

'They're not quite what I thought they would be,' he said, and escaped.

Nowadays they would probably fetch what she asked at the beginning, but even then, when prices were so very low, the verdict of a dealer acquaintance was surely most unkind. . . .

'Eight quid the bloody lot!'

The second reply, which I believe came the week after, threw me into wild excitement. Another lady wrote to say she had 'over fifty small cabinet pieces,' all quite perfect, and all beautifully decorated. She was not asking a high price because she had no room to keep them.

This was in the middle of the week, and I wrote to say that since she lived nearly fifty miles away I would call on the following Saturday afternoon.

The rest of the week was purgatory. I could not get those pieces out of my mind! What could they be? Dainty little Derby mugs painted with miniature landscapes by Boreman? Jewelled vases from Flight's of Worcester painted by Baxter? All these I knew. Or could they possibly be, was it too wildly fantastic to hope that they might be Chelsea 'toys'?

Saturday came at last. I arrived in my car within a stone's throw of the house in time to eat my sandwiches. They stuck in my throat. The hands of my watch crept slowly round to dead on two o'clock, and within five minutes I was knocking at the door.

She was a pleasant woman and she had a lovely home. I saw many pieces I would have loved to own, but she steered me resolutely past them to throw open the door of a small room.

'There!' she exclaimed, triumphantly.

There, indeed! Spread out upon a Chippendale pie-crust table was a fine collection of Goss 'armorial' china.

I do not know whether it included 'A Present from Margate,' for I did not stay to look.

That very true and dismal story reminds me that this kind of chancy buying can sometimes have very different results. A dealer I knew well had a lovely home in Broadway. He was an educated man who in retirement had managed to persuade the local council that there was room for just one more antique shop in that overrated but still beautiful village.

Like most dealers, he had his own little den, in this case a loft across the back yard, approached by a rickety outside stairway. Here he kept some most unusual things. I had not known him very long when he showed me a little Battersea gem, a patch-box, the lid enamelled with a miniature landscape. Inside was a tiny mirror. But (and this was the point), between the two was a false lid upon which was enamelled a very naughty picture indeed!

How many similar boxes, I wonder, are displayed in all innocence, the trick of the catch unsuspected, on many a chaste drawing-room mantelpiece or table?

Also not for public view was a beautifully painted chamber-pot. On the outside were English flowers, but on the bottom, inside of course, was a lifelike, full-size portrait of Napoleon. What made matters worse was the fact that his mouth was wide open!

This preamble may show that here was a man with a twinkle in his eye, though of this side of his character there could have been no sign when one day he was invited by two maiden ladies to make an offer for a pair of very fine K'hang H'si vases. Or, at least, so they had been given to understand by their father, who had recently died.

They entered the drawing-room together, and there on the high Adam mantelpiece, pushed back close against the chimney-breast, were the vases, of baluster shape and about 10 inches in height. There was no doubt about their provenance or their quality. He thought to himself, K'hang H'si *famille verte*. Now, what about the price!

He crossed the floor for a closer view, but as he did so one of the sisters touched his arm.

'Please, Mr. P., do you mind not touching the vases?' she said, rather confusedly, he thought.

So he stood before the fireplace with his hands clasped behind his back, and looked most carefully at the left-hand vase. Flowering shrubs, rocks, and birds, the colours brilliant and fresh, and the faint iridescence around the blue enamel. No damage of any kind, at least not on the side he could see.

Without thinking he stretched out his hand and lifted the vase from its place.

A sudden shriek almost caused him to drop it. He turned quickly, just in time to see the crimson blush which flooded both the sallow faces before the sisters turned tail and fled from the room!

Only then, disconcerted and not a little mystified, did he look at the other side of the vase.

The picture painted upon it was even more disgraceful than that upon his patch-box lid!

It was only with difficulty that he persuaded the ladies to discuss business. This at last they did with averted looks. The subject of the decoration made the vases cheap at £250, but he had to do his own packing.

Yes, the dealer gets his chances, but the collector does better to get out and about. He finds more, and he learns so much.

Naturally enough, he makes mistakes.

Among the many which I myself made in the early days was the purchase of a set of Oriental 'rice-grain' bowls and covers from a shop in Shrewsbury. The technique used in this class of ware was to pierce a pattern of crescents and ovals through the unfired clay, which was of course filled in with the glaze. The result is that the pattern is revealed when the ware is held against the light.

I bought the set because I had recently seen and handled some Chinese examples, painted in underglaze blue in just the same way. So far as I could see in the rather dimly-lit shop every piece was quite perfect. The dealer obligingly packed them neatly in a cardboard box, and I rejoiced in a bargain.

Only when I arrived home did I find that they were Japanese, grey in paste and so thick in glaze that the decoration was quite blurred.

I wondered then, and I take it as a warning now, how much a year did he make by having an ill-lit shop?

They say that opportunity never knocks but once. How true it is! One evening, just as it was getting dusk, I called to see a dealer who no sooner than I had entered his shop produced from a drawer a little Chinese 'Dog of Fo' in rock crystal. Alertness and savagery were in every carved line, and the price was £5.

Cheap, I thought, and so it was. But then, it was dusk, and bearing in mind my 'rice-grain' disaster I saw that the crystal looked rather cloudy, and recalled that clouded crystal is not so acceptable as the clear. So I postponed my decision until the following afternoon. Of course, it had gone.

Time and time again I say to beginners, 'If you see a thing and like it, buy it there and then! If you don't, someone else will get in first!' And yet, knowing this to be true, I myself can never learn.

I remember when my wife and I called in a little shop in Cheltenham, kept by a mother and daughter who are invariably charming and who always have something good and reasonably priced to show me. They had been to a sale of Chinese furnishings and apparently had enjoyed themselves. A great sideboard, massive and heavily padlocked, almost filled one side of the shop, Buddhas and goddesses of all shapes and sizes, in soapstone, bronze, and porcelain occupied every inch of table-top and shelves, and the display of silks and brocades was worthy of Libertys itself. It was all very lovely and very cheap. 'Chinese rubbish!' most of the dealers had said. And in the window, restrained and shapely, was a little low table, its top up-curving at either end, and doubtless intended for use at the tea-drinking ceremony.

We were looking for a coffee-table as it happened, and this seemed to be just what we wanted. But was not £10 too much to pay for an everyday piece of furniture? Yet it was cheap, for what it was. But would it live at peace with our oak? We hummed and hawed, decided against it, and left the shop.

Not a hundred yards along the street I stopped the car. 'Get out!' I exclaimed to my wife. 'Walk back quickly, buy it, and I'll turn the car and join you in a minute!'

She hurried off, and met me with a long face in the shop doorway.

'A gentleman came in just as we left and has bought it!' she said.

Never, NEVER, miss an opportunity. Others too have eyes to see.

Such occurrences are only some of the many disappointments which beset the path of every collector. Glowing second-hand reports are often misleading, and the average person cannot understand that rarity is not enough. I do not know who was the more disappointed, my friend who told me that he had 'found' a pair of vases in an attic, or I when I went to see them. They had been his father's, and had been in the family 'for hundreds of years.'

I went to see them. Immediately I recognized the scale-blue, the painted views in scrolled reserves, and the soft, raised gilding.

Early Worcester, about 1775, I told him, and ought to be worth a lot of money, for they were at least 18 inches high.

Unfortunately for both of us, rare though they were, the bottoms of both had been knocked out, mere shells, and poor at that. Almost cause for tears.

Modern collectors have good reason to lament a tragedy of another kind—the enhanced value of every kind of antique. One book, indeed, which describes the fascinating experiences of the most famous and successful collector of all time, Lady Charlotte Schreiber, should never be read by anyone who wishes to preserve peace of mind!

This remarkable lady began to collect in middle life, and she scoured the Continent for rare pieces fifty-odd years ago. The prices she paid were ludicrous, as may be seen if they are studied before visiting the actual specimens in the Victoria and Albert Museum.

Even I, looking back less than half that space of time, lament that I was not better breeched while there was still a little time.

It was my custom to keep a sort of diary of my 'finds,' with prices paid, and brief comments of condition and so on. Here is a typical page.

Salt-glaze tea-bowl and saucer, enamelled flowers, lovely and perfect	£6	10	0
Liverpool porcelain bowl, 7 inches, painted with Chinese scene and marked with initials of Zachariah Barnes, brilliant and colourful	£6	0	0
Worcester leaf-dish, moulded 'Blind Earl' pattern, printed in black with Hancock's *L'Amour*. Too dear?	£3	5	0
Worcester cream-jug, helmet shape, snake handle, painted with flowers, raised trident mark on shoulder	£3	10	0
Whieldon pottery leopard, with coloured glazes	£3	10	0
Worcester tea-bowl, polychrome coat-of-arms		12	6
Coalport plate, portrait of W. G. Grace, dated 1895	£2	0	0
Bow white figure of a lion, harmonious	£6	10	0

I wish I had them now!

By and large, as I have already suggested, the friendly dealer who is willing to 'keep a look out' is the collector's best friend. And what a varied, amazing, cosmopolitan, democratic fellowship it is to which he belongs! I know collectors who are schoolmasters, fish-and-chip fryers, postmen, water-bailiffs, insurance brokers, and signalmen, and apparently on the least provocation any one of them may decide quite suddenly to join the ranks of those whose fathers were dealers before them.

I had collected scarcely a year when I first met the late William Braithwaite of Worcester. He was as much an institution as the Edgar Tower which overshadowed his shop. He told me, on learning that I was a schoolmaster, that he had once been a woodwork instructor, who had turned antique dealer as the result of a nervous breakdown. The sort of gossip which we used to enjoy is meat and drink to all collectors.

At first he solemnly warned me against the wicked ways of his own trade. With a twinkle in his eye he told how he himself had once conspired with a brother craftsman to make innumerable long-case clocks which sold like hot cakes in the London salerooms. I suspect that the tale was invented to prove to me that the sharp London fellows were not so sharp, after all!

This led to a more serious story which he assured me was perfectly true.

One day a dealer sold a fine set of Hepplewhite chairs to a wealthy peer. They were graceful and well-proportioned, slenderly strong, beautifully carved and of mellow colour. They seemed to be all they pretended to be, but in fact they were fakes.

Sure enough the purchaser called in a museum expert who condemned them out of hand.

Furious, the nobleman complained to the dealer, who expressed his surprise and regret, offering at the same time to take them back. Somewhat mollified, his disappointed client accepted a cheque and agreed to sign a receipt for it, a receipt for the sum of so many hundreds of pounds for 'A set of Hepplewhite chairs,' suitably (but not too accurately) described.

Some weeks later an American millionaire called in, saw the chairs, and fell in love with them. There was only one thing, had they a history? Where did they come from?

'I bought them only a few weeks ago from Lord So-and-so,' said the dealer. 'See, here is the receipt!'

That clinched it! The chairs travelled across the Atlantic, and I suppose they are still there.

'I wouldn't trust some of them an inch,' said my friend. 'Would you believe it, I told old what's-his-name only last week about a refectory table which I thought might do for a client of his. "Buy it for me on commission," says he. And like a fool I told him where it was! The next day as I went down one drive of the big house I caught sight of him going hell-for-leather down the other! I only beat him to it by a short head!'

One day he showed me a Chelsea figure he had just bought privately, for he never attended sales. It was a lovely, graceful thing, but quite beyond my pocket. As usual, he did not mind.

He just liked to show it to me. He caressed the soft glaze lovingly before returning it to its cabinet. One thing led to another, and at last he said to me, 'Did I ever tell you about the cat and the Chelsea?'

I replied that he had not, and for a few moments his thoughts were evidently far away. Then he chuckled, and went on:

'Just after my breakdown, when I was still very nervy but fit enough otherwise, a lady wrote to ask me to go to see and perhaps to buy a collection of Chelsea figures which she could not afford to keep. I arrived at her home, a country vicarage, late one close, thundery afternoon, told my driver to wait for me, and hurried to the door to miss the heavy spots of rain which were just beginning to fall.

'She took me straight up to a first-floor room so dark that I could scarcely see across it, but in a moment I could just make out the ghostly white shapes of the groups and figures which crowded the mantelpiece and the top of a grand piano in a far corner. There must have been at least twenty of them.

'No sooner had I begun to step across the room to make a closer examination than the threatened storm broke in earnest. A terrific clap of thunder fairly shook the house, and a vivid lightning-flash lit the room as bright as day. I glanced anxiously at the window, to see only a few yards away, in the churchyard, the long rows of white tombstones.

'That did it! With a hasty word of apology I quitted the room and stumbled down the dark stairway.

'Full of concern the lady followed me, and I made my explanations. Could I come again, the following day perhaps, in the morning? So it was arranged, and I ran through the pouring rain to my car.

'When I came once more to the house my client met me on the doorstep with a worried face. She said not a word, but beckoned me in, and led the way, still silent, up the staircase.

'She stood to one side and motioned me to enter the room.

'Never shall I forget the sight that met my eyes!

'The room was pleasant and light in the morning sun, but where were the groups and figures I had come to buy? They were no longer there, but the floor was littered with broken arms and legs, heads, and shapeless fragments of china. The mantelpiece was quite bare, but on the piano stood one solitary little cupid, gazing down sadly at his own reflection.

'I looked inquiringly, anxiously, at my companion. For a moment she could not utter a word. Her throat worked convulsively. Then:

' "Oh, Mr. Braithwaite," she gulped, "isn't it terrible? It's all that miserable cat. When we left last night we must have locked her in, and the thunder drove her quite wild. This is the result! What can we do?"

'Well, there was nothing we could do, and so I explained. I sympathized as best I could, though I felt pretty down-in-the-mouth myself, and made the best of a bad business by buying the cupid.'

An honest dealer who never attends sales is usually in demand when anyone has something to sell, or when a valuation is needed. I once asked Braithwaite whether there was still much to be found in the remoter country houses, and he told me the story of yet another strange experience which will bear repetition.

It appears that an insurance company had asked him to make an inventory of the contents of a large mansion near Pershore, where lived an old lady all alone save for her old butler and his wife. Rather unwillingly, because he was suffering from a heavy cold, he rang for a car, gave the driver the instructions the company had given as regards the whereabouts of the place, and off they set in the pouring rain on the nine-mile journey.

Now, if he had not had a cold, and if the car windows had not been obscured by the rain, Braithwaite would probably have taken note of the route. As it was, he wrapped himself in a rug and made himself as comfortable as possible on the back seat. He knew only that the driver lost his way several times before at length they drew up before the entrance porch of a Queen Anne house of some size.

The old butler had expected him, and explained that he was free to go where he would. He then disappeared through a green baize door into his own quarters.

Braithwaite first entered a great drawing-room, and immediately forgot his cold and his petulance in amazement at what he saw. The tapestries upon the walls were so fine as to be completely outside his experience, but it did not take him long to estimate the value of the furniture, the glass, the pictures, and the china at a sum not far short of £10,000.

That first room set the standard for the entire place. When at last he made his way into the basement, more out of curiosity than anything else, he found store cupboards crammed full of Waterford glass. In a conservatory he found flower-pots, their contents withered, resting in Worcester plates and saucers decorated in scale-blue and claret and green, painted exquisitely with Chinese figures, exotic birds, and flowers.

His task completed, he rang for the butler, who showed him to the door. He was a man of few words, but Braithwaite dragged out of him that the old lady, so far as he knew, had no relations.

Such, then, was the story. I asked him, where was this wonderful house?

'Do you know,' said he, 'I have no idea. I've looked for it several times since, without success. The driver has no idea, because he got lost so many times. I don't even know its name! I did take the trouble to ring up the insurance company some months later, only to be told that the old lady had left the district. I suppose she took everything with her, but if she did there'll be a wonderful sale somewhere, some time!'

What would a collector give for the *entrée* to a place of that kind!

Every dealer has a place where he stores his forgotten rubbish, and every collector hopes that one day he may be able to explore it. Braithwaite had cellars, a shed, and an attic. The cellars were full of old oak; panels (some of them priceless 'linenfold'), planks, carved overmantels and bed-boards, and beams, all hoarded up awaiting some most improbable use. From his shed, an old disused 'tin chapel' some yards down the street, I bought two Chippendale folding fire-screens with slender, turned legs and pierced frets (at a pound each, as I remember), two old harps, and several sets of dresser shelves. In the attic I unearthed an enormous

Georgian convex mirror. Although some of the golden balls were missing and the great, flaunting eagle had lost its beak I would have bought it for a matter of shillings had I thought I could have got it down the steep, narrow staircase. But behind it, stacked against the wall, I found a set of six French prints—I remember *La Rixe* was one of them—in chipped wood and carved gesso frames of good quality. Braithwaite stood back as I raised a cloud of dust, and deplored the ruin of my clothes. I took no notice, and carried them out one by one to where the landing skylight threw a little more light. He came closer then, and picked up one of them gingerly.

'Those used to belong to Duveen,' he said, 'and I think they might be good. I've never taken the trouble to find out.'

'How much?' I asked.

'Six pounds to you,' he replied, 'but I don't say they're right!'

When I got home I took them out of their frames and sent them straight off to Sothebys for an opinion. The verdict came in a few days. Good quality fakes!

I had the frames repaired and regilded, and passed the set on to a dealer for £25.

On the staircase which led up to the attic there were many pictures, most of them steel engravings, but including also a rather large oil-painting of a woman which hung there to my knowledge for many years. Its details were hidden by the filth of many more, but at least it had a good frame! One day I paused for a closer look.

'I think it's good,' said my old friend, 'and I gave £10 for it twenty years ago. The London men have seen it and turned it down.'

I knew and still know nothing about pictures, and I forgot the incident until one day, I think it was in 1937, he greeted me with a rueful smile.

'Remember that picture, the one on the staircase? Well, it's gone! So-and-so from Hereford bought it for what I gave. Had it cleaned and it's gone to America. What do you think it turned out to be? A genuine Titian, and it's been up there for twenty years!'

That was all. No complaints. Just the luck of the game, and another proof that knowledge pays dividends!

Braithwaite was one of those dealers who are never afraid to buy. Not because they know what something is, but because they have a flair for recognizing quality when they see it. Not so many years ago, just before he died, in fact, I was looking for nice pieces of oak to furnish one room of my Georgian house. I had an idea that the tin chapel might have possibilities, but the first thing that met my eye in the shop itself was a large oak cabinet on stand. I suppose it was about 4 feet in width and nearly 6 feet high, but its outstanding feature was the colourful enamelling of the plaques which covered the front of every small drawer. There must have been at least a dozen of them.

'What's this?' I asked.

'What do you think?' countered Braithwaite.

'I've not the least idea,' said I. 'Surely it can't be English?'

'That's what everybody says!' was the reply. 'The London men who have seen it all say it's Italian, but I have an idea it's English. Any use to you?'

'How much?' I then asked. It certainly was a stately piece!

'Seventy-five pounds, and I still say it's English!'

I hivered and hovered. It was rather large, and the panels were after all rather gaudy. Would it live with my cottage pieces? And could I spare £75 for something I could well do without? I decided I could not.

Now hear the sequel!

Two or three months later I paid another visit. I rang the little bell which stood on a table in the entrance lobby at the foot of the stairs, and Braithwaite opened the door of his private room. He beckoned me in.

'Found me any oak?' I asked.

There was no reply for a moment. Then he took the current number of the *Connoisseur* from a drawer, opened it at the centre double page, and handed it to me.

'Look at that. Ever seen it before?'

Well, there as large as life was a photograph of the puzzle piece, and the announcement by a world-famous London dealer of the recent purchase of a 'unique and early example of English furniture,' fitted with contemporary enamelled plaques by an Italian master!

The price asked (and quickly got, so I am told) ran into four figures!

We looked at each other.

'Don't you wish you'd had it for £75?' said Braithwaite.

It appeared that a provincial dealer had backed his opinion, and straightway passed the piece on to London for several hundreds of pounds.

Every collector lives in hope of a find of this kind, but he is usually disappointed. All the same, he is unlucky indeed if he never comes across something good.

Tipping and I set off one Saturday morning for the Cotswolds. We paused in Burford and Stowe and found nothing of consequence. 'How about Bath?' asked Con, 'or do you think it's too far?'

I did not think so, and Bath it was, with a fruitless call in Cirencester on our way. We parked the car, looked in at Mallet's window but did not go in, and made a bee-line for the back streets, finding nothing until at length we stopped before the grimy window of a small, single-roomed shop, against which we pressed our noses.

It was one of those places which are half-way between an 'antique gallery' and a junk-shop. Its dimness hinted at possibilities, for although the window itself held nothing we coveted, what there was appeared to be of good quality and in good condition. Furthermore, we could catch the gleam of china behind the dusty glass of the several cabinets which stood against the dingy walls.

It is a great mistake to suppose that an unkempt shop is a sign of low prices! I have learnt by experience, sometimes embarrassing, that when some shirt-sleeved, unshaven dealer produces a piece from a crowded hotch-potch of a cabinet he likely as not prices it just as highly as would a Bond Street connoisseur. Nevertheless, one can always hope.

'Shall we go in?' said Con.

'May as well,' I replied.

He removed his hearing aid and in we went. A little bell over the door tinkled, but for a few moments nothing happened. Then a curtain behind a glass panel in a door at the back of the shop was drawn stealthily aside, and a young woman's face peered out at us. Apparently reassured, she came out.

Could we look round, we asked.

She hesitated. Then 'Well, I suppose so,' she said, 'but it is rather difficult. You see, the shop belonged to my mother-in-law and she died last week. My husband and I want to sell up and get back to our own home, but I'm afraid we don't know what anything is worth!'

Tipping looked inquiringly at me. I opened my mouth, which was my signal that I wanted him to hear something I had to say.

On went the hearing aid, a tap against the waistcoat pocket microphone, and I explained the position.

Not a muscle of his face changed. He turned to the woman and set to work. Never had he been so persuasive as he asked about the dead lady's complaint, her symptoms, her family, their family, their plans, and everything that was theirs. Finally (and all the time my eyes were exploring every corner of the little shop), he asked if she would trust us to make a fair offer for anything we fancied.

She agreed! She even asked if she might return to her cooking while we looked round, and we replied that that would suit us very nicely.

No sooner was her back turned than we set to work. And by that I do mean WORK, for the examination of antiques of any kind calls for the utmost concentration, and for the instantaneous remembering of every scrap of knowledge ever gained from books and from experience. Every cabinet was ransacked, every drawer pulled out, and every pile of dirty plates taken apart one by one.

Not together, mind! It was our friendly understanding that our hunting was on the basis of each man for himself, and it was up to each of us, if he could, to sum up the possibilities of every nook and cranny before the other could get round to it!

In the space of an hour or so we found many desirable pieces, which we gathered together in two groups on a table-top. We decided upon prices which though fair were yet such as we would be glad to pay. Then we tapped on the door. The young woman agreed to everything we suggested, and before long we were walking to my car with our arms and pockets full of little parcels.

I suppose this experience must be almost unique, and looking back I know that we ought to have come away with much more. It sticks in my mind that Con clutched a white Bow group to his breast, among other lovely things, and my raincoat pocket bulged with a Worcester tea-pot and cover, black-printed by Hancock with Panini Ruins and enamelled by Giles.

We made record time on our journey home through Stroud and Painswick, knowing that the best part of the day was still to come. After supper we shut ourselves up in the little study to unpack and discuss our finds, discovering fresh beauties and unsuspected virtues in every piece. For once it was not necessary for Con to give his usual caution: 'Whatever you do, don't tell the missus what I gave for this! That's between you and me. The women don't understand!'

The close comradeship of two collectors cannot easily be put into words. A fine piece is the touchstone of their friendship, the leaven, if you like, that brightens it and causes it to glow. It is something the layman cannot hope to understand, and when it is interrupted, as ours was so soon to be, collecting for a time loses its savour, only with difficulty and in the long course of time to be found again.

My diary reminds me that only a few weeks after this experience, in the summer of 1938, I had another lucky day, this time in a small Midlands town which in those days was always a happy hunting ground. A friend wrote to tell me that he had seen what he thought might be four large Chelsea figures in a junk-shop. He had not gone in, but had seen them through the window, standing on a table at the back of the shop. Was I interested?

Now this was on the Tuesday, and I knew that every Saturday morning the many antique shops in the town were thoroughly scoured by an army of ardent collectors, every one eager to outdo his fellows and to gloat right through the following week. There was no time to lose! No sooner had I closed my village school than I was on my way, and I entered the shop as the clock struck five.

The proprietress, whom I knew very well, was a very large, red-faced woman who always smelt strongly of drink. Like her father before her she was fairly knowledgeable, but could never afford to buy anything worth while, relying for the most part on selling for others on a small commission.

I saw immediately that the figures were still there, but at first I took no notice of them. For some minutes I picked my way through a horrible miscellany of old clothes, boots and shoes, broken domestic earthenware, stuffed birds in broken cases, mantelpiece ornaments, cheap jewellery, books, and sewing machines. All the time she watched me closely, relating meanwhile the most intimate details of her chronic ill-health.

('It's the wind wot serves me something cruel, dearie!')

Then, when at long last I picked up one of the figures, her face lit up.

'They're Chelsea, they are! And the gentleman won't take less than £10 for the set!'

A set of the Four Continents, each some 10 inches in height, and in mint condition, for £10!

Only, they were not Chelsea. The metallic gilding, the 'hard' paste, and the skimpy glaze all pointed to that arch-deceiver, Samson of Paris. Nevertheless, at that price I could not go wrong, and after, as in duty bound, I had half-heartedly tried to beat her down, the deal was done.

I left the shop with the figures wrapped in newspaper, and she followed close on my heels, doubtless to collect from her 'gentleman' and to seek the nearest pub.

I passed the set on to a dealer, who strangely enough refused to believe they were anything other than genuine Chelsea.

It would be quite wrong to think that much of Samson's work is anything other than of the highest quality. He was a genius, and his broad shoulders will stand all the condemnations which have been heaped upon them. He imitated, it is true, but every imitation is of something fine, and perfect in its way. It will one day be valuable, and some museums have devoted cabinets to it. I have owned a set of 'Derby' Mansion House dwarfs and several very large 'Worcester' cabbage-leaf jugs painted with exotic birds. All these were well-modelled and carefully painted, as was a stately straight-sided mug bearing the Plymouth tin symbol in gold, just as the dwarfs were marked with the crossed batons and crown, and the jugs with the blue square mark. I do not believe the claim that every piece made by Samson had a distinguishing mark.

I have often suggested that a valuable collection, and certainly an interesting one, might be made of first-class fakes. The reply might be made, perhaps, that one is landed with them often enough without looking for them.

Four

It occurs to me that in the course of the previous chapters I may have given the impression that the profession of antique dealing —for at its highest level it is a profession—is filled with rogues. Of course nothing could be farther from the truth, although it is unfortunately true that it has been entered by many who have no understanding or appreciation of old things, but who have not been slow to take advantage of a good thing. They use the slickness and the sharp business sense they have acquired in other trades to deal in those classes of antiques which are in immediate demand. During the later war years the Americans clamoured for 'modern' Worcester. Their shop-windows were full of it in no time. Then came the craze for 'Dresden' figures and for Royal Dux, the bigger the better, and in stepped the 'wide boys' once more. Now, as I write, it is the turn of 'cameo glass,' and in a year's time it will be something else.

Occasionally, often by mistake, this sort of dealer comes by a really old piece, which looks out of place amongst its gaudy, nineteenth-century neighbours. Along comes a collector who, if he does not buy it, is kind enough to identify it.

'That ought to be in a cabinet,' says he. 'Don't you know what it is?' And so the next customer comes in, and it is offered to him as a 'collector's piece,' as if anything worth while were not in that category!

This is the sort of dealer who ships to America, and of course reputable dealers have to follow suit. I shall not quickly forget seeing a large oak refectory table in a well-known dealer's dining-room, the top of which was crammed with china and glass awaiting packing and shipment. Fortunately, we have got rid of a great deal of rubbish in this way, but our cousins over the water are quick to learn, and with discrimination will come the danger that in years to come we may well be sending agents to America to buy back our treasures. It is perhaps not generally known that of recent years Chinese collectors have been buying up fine porcelain, ivory, and jade which their less wise ancestors allowed to leave their country.

The British Antique Dealers' Association sees to it that the hard, reliable core of the profession is undisturbed, and every collector is the better for its vigilance. Its members are governed by strict rules based on honest dealing, which does not mean that any such supervision is by any means always necessary.

Some time before the outbreak of war Tipping and I found a new shop in a Gloucestershire town. In the window, which bore the B.A.D.A. medallion, was some good coloured Bristol delft, several pieces of Sheffield Plate and silver, and a case of jewellery, and through it we could see some well-kept furniture.

We entered, and after a few minutes' conversation with the tall, stooping, rather saturnine proprietor we knew that he had once been in Duke Street, London, had lost a lot of money in the slump, and had come to Gloucestershire with nothing but a fine stock of goods and an expert knowledge of furniture, plate, silver, and jewellery.

For a time things were difficult, but every time we called there were signs of increasing prosperity, and more and more emphasis on pottery and porcelain, which he had begun to study. Accordingly, when I decided in 1937 to sell all my oddments and to specialize he offered to buy them, or to exchange them for anything I fancied from his stock.

I took my pieces in several large boxes, having priced them, as I thought, suitably. We laid them all out on a table in his tiny back room. He examined each piece and agreed to take them all off my hands. We totted up the prices.

Then 'This isn't enough!' he exclaimed.

And to my amazement and pleasure he suggested a considerably higher sum. More, for among the pieces was a certain

Oriental wine-pot, shaped like a peach, green and purplish-brown in colour, and filled through a hole in the base on the principle of an unspillable ink-well. The well-known 'Cadogan' pots in brown earthenware, made at Rockingham and by Mintons, were imitations of similar pieces.

Now, if the piece were truly Chinese it was valuable, but if, as I suspected, it were a Japanese copy, then its value was about what I had paid for it, which was fifteen shillings.

'I'll tell you what I'll do,' said he. 'I'll give you your price, but if I can sell it to an expert who accepts it as "right," at a proper price, then I'll share with you.'

Such honest dealing deserved the success which he later had as an expert on old English porcelain, and it is sad to think that illness has laid him low, and that he is forced to carry on business from his private home, and from his bed.

Just as I am often heartened by the memory of this and other similar incidents, so am I happy in the ever fuller realization of the wide horizons which have been opened out to me in the pursuit of my hobby. Collecting can never be a solitary pursuit. Not, that is, if its fullest savour is to be enjoyed, although I am well aware that there are some who seem to be content to gloat in solitude over their possessions. For myself, I must show them, talk about them, and even write about them. And above all I cannot help but rejoice in the human contacts which collecting has brought to me, and in the scenes and places into which it has led my steps. It is not so much the goal that matters, but what one sees and finds on the way.

On a lucky day I decided to spend a short summer holiday in a tiny Cotswold town. The intention was to fish the mayfly on the Colne and Windrush, but I was too late, and had ample time to prove, instead of trout-streams, the more mellowed fascinations of the antique shops. The inn where I was lodging was an old coaching house built of somewhat incongruous red brick, but across the square was another large building, long and low, built of golden Cotswold stone. Two large boards, one on either side of the little entrance porch, above the ground-floor windows, bore the words 'ANTIQUES' and 'DECORATIONS,' and both night and day the orange and red light from modern but shapely Venetian lanterns revealed just enough of the treasures within to tempt one to go inside. I learnt from the locals that the place had once been yet another coaching house (strange how these tiny Cotswold villages could support so many of them!), that it had then been used for many years as the rectory, and that now, for some time, it had been the property of an antique dealer from London. I could find out very little about him, save that he was apparently honest. Of course he was a 'foreigner,' and the villagers were not particularly interested.

Purposely I delayed my first visit until the middle of the week, by which time I would know whether or not I had any money to spare. On the Wednesday morning I went in, and was greeted pleasantly enough by a short, bearded man who introduced himself as John Havinden. I liked him at once, and when I had told him about my books and articles, some of which he had read, we fell to talking. We walked from room to room, opening a cabinet here and picking up a figure there. In answer to his request that I should give my opinion on some of his pieces I said that I would be only too pleased, and he smiled wryly. 'The trouble about you experts is that you will never commit yourselves!' he exclaimed. 'Expert is a bad word,' I answered. 'It's natural that the pieces you show us are bound to be those upon which many different opinions are possible! I do not claim to be an expert, but I've handled so many pieces that it is quite possible that what is a problem piece to you may well be known to me. After all, you cannot expect to have anything like a comprehensive knowledge of every class of antique in your shop unless you are a specialist, which is just what I try to be!' And of course, as I expected, I was shown several services that might well have been Swansea but that might equally well have been made at Coalport. 'A well-known Swansea collector told me these were quite definitely "right",' said my new friend. 'What do you think?' I could only reply that if he chose to sell them as such neither I nor anyone else could prove him to be wrong. I saw, too, an exquisite little figure in white porcelain, bearing the Derby crossed batons and crown in overglaze blue, and could only agree that its too hard paste betrayed it as yet another Samson masterpiece. So it went on, an hour of the kind of debate, and argument and reasoning that collectors love, until at length I left, having promised to call in again for coffee after dinner the following Friday evening.

I remember that I caught several suicidal trout during the Friday afternoon, and the experience, followed by a good dinner and a bottle of claret, put me into good mood for my evening engagement. I found the front door open, and before long found myself being introduced to the lady of the house, who immediately rushed away again to put her three children to bed, the while Havinden and I explored the garden. How I love these walled Cotswold gardens, even though this one was to some extent spoiled by the slate roof which some vandal (surely not the departed rector!) had caused to be placed upon one of the several outhouses. I thought of Crowther when we paused to admire the statues that stood here and there, and I swear that one of them smiled, a little coyly but still appreciatively, as I stroked her cold, mossy flank in passing. But then, quite dispelling my fancy, there were three warmer smiles from a landing window, and pell-mell across the lawn rushed three little figures in blue dressing-gowns, their faces blushing from the bath, to bid their father goodnight. The chores were over, the laughter faded along the corridors, and my hostess was free to lead me to the promised coffee and to a comfortable Georgian settee upon which I was invited to put up my feet if I felt like it.

Perhaps it was the brandy, following so soon upon the claret, or perhaps it was the warmth of my welcome. Perhaps it was the antique furniture that surrounded us. Or was it, perhaps, that the common bond of collecting always breaks down reserve and invites confidence as nothing else can? I learned at any rate that my host had turned to dealing as a relief from film-making, and that his wife had been an artist. That I should have guessed from the many pictures that hung upon the walls and leaned against them, all betraying the same touch, and a feminine one at that. And so we talked, and put the world to rights until the dimming, one by one, of the bright lights in the hotel windows across the way warned me that all good things must come to an end. I had gone to look at antiques, and perhaps to buy, and instead I had met yet two more of those nice people whom collecting attracts into its fold.

I have spoken of fishing, and I am reminded that this pastime has often gone hand in hand with my other. Some years ago a friend decided that a certain old traction engine, that he had found standing forlorn and rusting in the lee of a Cotswold barrow, ought to be brought into Worcestershire, there to end her days in honourable retirement. How to get her home. By road, of course, under her own steam, and following the byways. That it would take at least five days to cover the ninety-odd miles did not matter, and several most enjoyable days were spent in prospecting a likely route. This is not the place to talk about the actual journey, about how our adventures were a nine days' wonder in the Press and on the radio, and about how we arrived home at length as black as niggers, in the pouring rain at well after midnight, but feeling better than we had felt for years! That is all another story. What does matter is that we arranged to lodge for one night at Temple Guiting, where there was a quiet old guest-house perched on a terrace above the winding Windrush.

'Any fish in the river?' I asked the proprietor.

'Not now, I'm afraid,' he replied. 'There used to be, for the water is dammed into three wide stretches and used to be well stocked, but it has not been fished for at least six years. See, here's the fish book.'

He produced the old book, and there was the evidence of frequent re-stockings, and of the catching of many trout, some of them up to nearly four pounds in weight.

There and then I decided to spend a week at the guest-house, later in August, and to take a rod.

The very first evening, after dinner, I strolled down to the water, rod in hand, not troubling to take my net, for if I caught anything at all I certainly expected nothing of any size. The shadows of the elms were long across the water-meadows, and the water was mirror smooth, almost stagnant, and undisturbed by any sort of ripple or splash.

Idly, almost carelessly, I made my first cast, and instantly there was a swirl and my rod bent like a bow! Five minutes later—it had to be that long because my net was in my bedroom—I was admiring a fat brown trout of nearly two pounds weight, the first of many I caught during the week. I was too busy, for once, even to think about junk-shops.

The following year the house was empty, and there was no fishing. Then, a year ago, I happened to see in *Country Life* an announcement by a firm of auctioneers to the effect that it had been sold. Straightway I wrote to their London address, enclosing a letter to the new tenant, whoever he might be. In it I told my experiences in the little river, and I mentioned, too, the fact that apart from fishing I was interested in ceramics, and had written about them. Why I did so I do not know, but I was delighted a few days later to receive a friendly letter from the new owner. Yes, he knew that he had bought a good stretch of fishing, though he himself was a beginner, and he intended to do a great deal of re-stocking. What was more, he had a copy of my latest book, and if I cared to go over to autograph it and to see some fine Derby dessert ware I was at liberty to cast a fly over the water. Be sure I needed no second invitation. Is it not strange how one thing leads to another?

I suppose I should never have proved the by-lanes of Wiltshire but for George Prangley.

Con Tipping and I heard, quite by accident, of a village postmaster who was a collector who sometimes sold a piece or two. He lived at a place of which I had never heard, a few miles beyond Cirencester, called Ashton Keynes.

That was enough! Letters passed, and the upshot was that one Saturday morning we set off to 'Ciren,' where we had lunch, and then to the flat little village whose only fame seemed to be founded upon a strange brotherhood who lived there, and who had all things in common. We saw a few of them as we approached the first few straggling cottages, sturdy, bearded fellows in brown homespun and sandals, who gave us good day and minded their own business.

We found the post office easily enough. Prangley was behind his counter, a tall, well-built man, ruddy of face and with a large walrus moustache. He bade us welcome in a slow, careful voice, left his married daughter to take care of business and took us into his sitting-room.

The first thing a collector does when he visits another for the first time is to spy out the land, as it were. His eyes dart around the first room he enters. Has this fellow got anything? Am I wasting my time? Rude it may be, but it is nevertheless all too true!

First impressions in this case were not at all promising. On the high mantelpiece was a nice, clean pair of early Worcester sauce-boats, moulded in the form of lettuce-leaves, with crabstock handles, and painted with fruit and insects. A late Japanese figure stood in the tiny window, and on the walls hung several Victorian papier-mâché fans, and a post-horn or two in gleaming copper and brass. The furniture was of heavy, red mahogany, and a dilapidated arm-chair stood at one side of the hearth.

Into this the old man sank with a sigh of relief, panting a little, having invited us to draw up a high chair apiece.

We talked about our journey, of the weather, and of the crops, and now and again he took snuff from a tiny Battersea box. Only when Tipping stood up at last, ostensibly to admire the sauce-boats, did the conversation get round to antiques. Then, with a vengeance, Prangley began to talk! Among other things we learnt that he had attended every local sale over a space of nearly forty years, buying up every piece of fine porcelain and glass upon which he could lay his hands. Often he had had little or no competition.

At last he stood up. Would we care to see his collection?

Would we not! Eagerly we followed into the next room, which was perhaps some 12 feet square, and the exact opposite of the room we had just left.

Here all was airy grace. The walls were colour-washed, the paintwork white, and picked out in gold. Dainty chintz curtains hung at either side of the two windows, on whose sills stood pots of flaming geraniums. The furniture, though typically Victorian of the drawing-room type, was yet slenderly graceful and fitting.

But the china! I do not exaggerate when I say that I have never seen finer or larger Chelsea groups than those which flanked the

Bow candelabra upon the mantelpiece. Three glazed cabinets, one of them of Dutch marquetry, were filled with Chelsea, Bow, and Worcester porcelain, figures, baskets, cream-jugs, sauce-boats, tea-pots, and complete tea-services decorated with scale-pattern, powder-blue, and ground colours of claret, apple-green, turquoise, and blue. And if that were not enough every spindly table carried its share of equally lovely, smaller pieces.

When we had looked at this piece and that, examining, discussing, and admiring, he led us to the door at the far end of the room.

'You'd better come and see the rest,' he said.

'What, is there still more?' asked Con, and raised his eyes and lifted protesting hands in his old familiar gesture of wonder and admiration.

We passed into a small hall or lobby, for the house had once been a little row of cottages, and this was a second entrance, now blocked up.

Everything here was 'blue and white,' which filled two cabinets. It was at about this time, in 1938, that I was falling in love with this restrained, simple ware, but before I could look my fill on he passed into the third and last room, which was clearly intended as an overflow, as it were, for the collection proper. Cabinets there were, though quite ordinary, painted deal affairs, but most of the pieces were hidden away in cupboards and in the drawers of a large oaken chest-upon-chest upon which stood an enormous 'Chinese Lowestoft' bowl, painted with a European fox-hunting scene. One of the cupboards was filled with glass, all of it old and much of it valuable, including specimens with airtwist and white and coloured twist stems.

You may be sure that the summer night was drawing in when at last we took reluctant leave of Prangley and his daughter, and made our way, empty-handed for once, back home.

This was the first of many visits, and always thereafter the old fellow let us take away a piece or two, though reluctantly. When he knew us better he took us upstairs, where on the landing stood a large case of 'blue and white' of the rarest kind, which he would not sell because his wife had been so fond of it.

The breathlessness we noticed on our first visit grew worse, and at last he had to give up the post office and his home. He was taken ill, and it was not expected that he would recover. However, the old man was tough, and one day I had a letter from Con in which he said, 'Last Friday a ring came from Prangley—a lady friend had two square-marked polychrome tea-pots—could I go over to see them? He couldn't describe patterns or name a price. It happened that evening that M—— dropped in for a rest and chat, and I told him. He said "I'll run you there on Monday!" We went through that awful rain in his ought-to-be-superannuated Austin 7, and got there about two-thirty. Prangley opened the door. Nearly his old self to look at, and keen. Poor on his pins, though, very short of breath, and doubtless feebler. Snuff-taking still a craze! He asked after you kindly. His old house is still vacant. He will see what he can do to get the cases down or across, and let me know when OUR turn comes! I suspect our pick-up days there are nearly done.'

So they were, for a few weeks later his daughter found him dead outside the door of their new home.

I should explain what Con meant by 'the cases.' We had known for some time that Prangley had packed away many of his early finds in large boxes which were now in the attic and had not been opened for many years. He could not even remember what was in them, and there was always an excuse when we suggested that we might perhaps help to refresh his memory by unpacking them! Either it was his anxiety lest we soil our clothes, or it was not worth our while, or some other reason, always in our best interests, of course, why the opening ought to be put off. Next time, perhaps, was ever the cry. And, of course, next time never came.

Tipping wrote to me giving me the news of his death.

'George Prangley died last Tuesday suddenly; his daughter phoned me to say so. I replied with an appreciatory letter of condolence and regret, and I associated you with my sympathies. He was a character and a gentleman. I am sorry I shall never see him again.'

Soon after this his daughter inquired whether we would like to go over to say what we thought of some china we hadn't seen before, and to make an offer for anything we liked.

The boxes at last! A date was fixed. We walked together from the new house to the post office, empty now, the garden sadly overgrown. The rooms were hardly changed, though the groups and candelabra were gone from the mantelpiece. Up the steep, narrow staircase, across the landing, and into a bedroom which was empty save for the china, all 'blue and white,' which littered the floor.

Left to ourselves, we took out paper and pencil. We identified and dated every piece, and set a reasonable price against it. I chose for myself, among other things, a pair of rare and beautiful Worcester chamber candlesticks and several straight-sided mugs. There were openwork baskets, egg-cups, and leaf-dishes of all kinds.

Our task done, we went downstairs, and handed over our lists.

None of the pieces ever came our way, after all. I have often wondered why. Was the reason, perhaps, that when a collector is used to buying at bargain prices he tends to undervalue his own pieces and those of others?

I know well that when George Prangley sold a piece a little vacant place was left in his heart. Nevertheless, we all do it, and I am sometimes asked, when I speak of having sold a fine piece, how could I bear to see it go? I have been asked, too, am I really a collector, or just another kind of dealer? And does not the 'trade' look askance at collectors who make a practice of buying to sell again, it may be at a profit?

What is really the truth of the matter, and where can one draw the line?

The true enthusiast is all too apt to spend more on his hobby than he can well afford. He may appease his own conscience, and his angry family, by insisting that his purchase is a wise investment, but at heart he knows that he is a weak-minded, improvident wastrel! So, time and time again, he sees a fine piece, is tempted, and invariably falls headlong. The result is that when he is financially embarrassed, as is all too often the case, it is a choice between a sale and the workhouse. I myself have painstakingly gathered together two fine collections, only to sell them again some years later for no other reason.

But there is, of course, another factor. It is better to have lived with a beautiful thing for a few months than never to have possessed it at all! For that reason a collector can enjoy much pleasant company at the cost only of a few hours of heartache when the time comes to part.

Sometimes he cheats himself. Many a 'private dealer' puts on a beloved piece a price-label so high that no one would ever think of buying it. Others hide a small collection away in their bedrooms, in case a tempting offer should prove their undoing.

I enjoyed the friendship and help of just such a private dealer for many years. He was one of the few who found so many good things that even the trade had to patronize him.

At the outset of a day's hunting one never knows what may be round the corner. I called on a certain dealer who had nothing for me, but as I was leaving he said casually, 'Do you know Glover, who lives in Worcester?'

I had never even heard of him, and said so. What was he, a dealer or a collector? I asked.

'A bit of both,' was the reply. 'He's a cunning old b—— and the boys hate the sight of him. Still, he's all right if you get to know him, and he gets some nice stuff.'

I wrote to the address I was given, and in due course was invited to see his collection. No mention of buying or selling was made on either side.

Albert Glover's house was the tiniest semi-detached council house I have ever seen, and certainly no one would ever have suspected what was inside, particularly as the curtains of the 'showroom' were always drawn of an evening before the lights were switched on.

I rang the door-bell, and after perhaps half a minute I heard a slow shuffle of footsteps. The door opened, and Glover, for it was he, led me past a modern grandfather clock on the one hand and a Victorian hall-stand on the other that almost filled the minute hall. The front room was not so very much bigger, certainly not more than 10 feet square, and in it was a large, modern draw-leaf table, a desk, a Dutch marquetry cabinet on stand, a bookcase standing upon a glass-fronted cupboard, a great show-case which entirely filled one wall, an easy chair, and two upright ones! The fireplace was almost hidden by a massive fire-screen of carved teak inset with blue-painted porcelain plaques. There was just enough room to walk carefully round the table, which was covered with china and glass of every description.

Glover himself was a short, powerful, very hairy man, spectacled, with a round, cheerful face and a discoloured, grizzled moustache. I could see as he walked before me that he limped badly. Whenever he was at home he discarded his jacket and his collar and tie. I was to find that he was a retired Post Office telegraph-line foreman, full of sound common sense and of a ready wit. Moreover, he loved beautiful things, had collected while still at work, and was now obliged to buy and sell to eke out his pension.

How that man adored china! Not so much the early ware, but the gaudier, more imposing vases and groups of the nineteenth century. Royal Dux and Dresden were his idea of perfection, and he had one great clock of the latter ware, covered with figures and flowers, which stood at least 2 feet high, and which was his pride and joy. 'Royal Worcester' he liked, too, and 'hard paste' Sèvres, painted plaques, and any kind of figures, provided they were perfect.

On my first visit I found every cabinet crammed with this kind of ware, and strange to say the little room was known to London dealers who visited him regularly. Seldom did he buy 'collector's pieces,' about which he knew little. I bought on this occasion a pair of tiny cups and saucers, decorated in the *famille rose* style with flowers, and a little covered bowl of that kind of Chinese steatitic porcelain that is sometimes wrongly called 'soft paste,' painted in underglaze blue with the 'Hundred Boys' pattern. These pieces he had bought in with other goods, and he had no idea what they were, though he recognized their fine quality and did not, of course, 'give them away'!

In collecting, as in business, it is often a case of 'every man for himself,' and it is foolish to give another the benefit of one's hardly earned experience to one's own disadvantage. On the other hand, I was often glad to be able to help Glover with pieces like those I have just mentioned, about which he knew nothing, and which I did not wish to buy. And, of course, he reciprocated by selling goods to me at a very small profit indeed.

One day when I called in he showed me a very fine oval basket, with pierced sides and handles moulded in the form of twisted rope. He always bought baskets of any kind, usually made at Rockingham, Coalport, or Dresden, but it needed only a glance to tell me that this was something quite different. It lacked the slickness, the accomplished potting, the bright glaze, and the brassy gold of late specimens. Its flower-painting was finely detailed, yet at the same time tentative, and its handles and rim were picked out in a pale blue enamel.

I held it up to the electric light, to find that the paste was very translucent, and white as the driven snow.

'What do you think it is?' I asked.

Glover shrugged his shoulders. 'I don't think it's English,' he said. 'German, perhaps, or even French. Anyway, it's a pretty piece and perfect. I expect I shall sell it all right.'

'So you ought,' said I, 'but mind you put a good price on it, for it was made at Pinxton by Billingsley, and it is a rare and valuable piece.'

Knowing that I was interested only in eighteenth-century wares, he sometimes did his best to find them for me, with the inevitable result that he was occasionally misled. He rang me up one evening with the news that he had just bought a very fine Worcester round basket, painted with flowers, that he thought I would like. The following Saturday afternoon round I went, and there it was on the table.

'What d'ye think of that for a piece?' he asked, smiling all over his face. 'I had a fight to get it, but I don't think I paid too much!'

'What did you pay?' I inquired.

'Ten pounds,' said he, 'and I'll let you have it for that, if you'll pay my expenses to Malvern.'

That certainly sounded cheap enough, and I stood there by the table and looked down at the piece without picking it up. About 10 inches in diameter, the sides pierced with crescents and fan-shapes, no handles, applied flowers on the outside, and the inside well-painted with English flowers.

So far, so good. I picked it up. And almost dropped it! It was as light as a feather!

Now this was all wrong, for it was thickly potted, and early Worcester is fairly heavy, though not as heavy as Bow. I turned it over, not to look for a mark, which I did not expect to find, but to look at the glaze inside the foot-rim, which I saw was thin and uniformly colourless, evenly spread over the creamy paste.

One test only remained. I held the piece up to the light, to find, as I feared, that it was completely opaque.

I put it sadly down on the table, and began to think what I ought to say.

At last, 'I'm terribly sorry, but I don't think I want it. You see, it isn't Worcester at all. It's Booth's earthenware, and a very clever copy.'

I often wonder, should one disillusion the proud possessor of a fake? If one does not, the odds are that someone else will. And yet ignorance is bliss, and an undetected fake gives the same pleasure as the genuine article. I suppose it all depends on circumstances. Many years ago I was admiring the wonders of a world-famous collection of porcelain when its owner called my attention to a cup and saucer decorated in Oriental style with mandarins and 'long elizas.'

'This is my latest acquisition,' said he proudly. 'So-and-so found it for me, and it's the finest copy of that kind of decoration I've ever seen. Notice how thinly it is potted. Go on! Take it out and examine it!'

I did so, gingerly. 'So-and-so' had stuck his trade label on the bottom. Certainly the potting was wonderful, and certainly the decoration left nothing to be desired. As my friend had pointed out, it was a wonderfully fine copy of the Chinese. Only, far from being English, it was a most blatant piece of Japanese porcelain, made I suppose not more than fifty years ago!

I replaced the cup and saucer in its place, and I fear my praise was somewhat faint. And in this instance I did not dare to give an opinion, for who was I to differ from a dealer and a collector both equally world-famous?

I would just say this, not for the first time. The collector who waits for his pieces to be found for him, and who accepts them at another's valuation, not only misses a lot of pleasure, but he also at the same time lays himself wide open to disillusion.

For many years Albert Glover attended the local sales, even sometimes travelling as far as Birmingham, Gloucester, or some other Midlands town. Sometimes by train or bus, sometimes by taxi, getting as close as possible to the place of the sale, and hobbling the rest of the way, painfully, slowly, his stick in one hand and a little black bag in the other. His coming was always quickly spotted by the members of the 'ring,' and how their faces fell when he entered the sale-room! They knew full well that if he wanted anything he would most likely have it, and that if they ran him too hard they would probably be 'left with the baby.' He often took an impish delight in raising the bidding on something he did not want, and he always knew just when to stop.

One day, a few years ago, he returned tired and weary from such a trip. It was a cold, wet day, and he had carried a heavy parcel of china for several miles through the pouring rain.

I saw him in bed a few weeks later, apparently fast recovering from his bout of bronchitis. He hoped to get downstairs the next day. So he did, and for a day or two he seemed to be making good progress. Then one evening, as he stood by his cluttered table, he staggered and fell. It was perhaps fitting, and completely in character, that with him in his fall he took down many of the pieces he so loved.

Here was an old man far removed from the popular idea of a collector, who yet had a real and understanding love for old and beautiful things that was far above mere knowledge of pastes and glazes, chemical analysis, and factory history. Truly, collecting leads one into a mixed company.

Strangely enough, his collection was not dispersed. While he was yet alive his family had shown little interest in his dealings—perhaps his enthusiasm was difficult to live with—but it was not very long after his death when his son began to turn up at the sales. We all know that the collecting bug is contagious, but perhaps it is hereditary too?

The year 1938 was for me a most eventful one. It was the beginning of my friendship with Glover, and in the June I paid my first visit to the Antique Dealers' Fair at Grosvenor House.

Owen Wheeler was manager, as I have already mentioned, and he suggested that I visit him there on the Saturday, so that he could show me around.

Naturally, I jumped at the chance. I knew that he had a suite of rooms in the hotel, and I looked forward to a few stolen hours of unwonted luxury and to meeting personalities whose galleries I had never dared to enter.

I travelled down on an early morning train, and my taxi took me straight to Park Lane in time for the morning opening. I passed the magnificent porter with as much assurance as I could muster, walked along the thickly-carpeted, softly-lit corridors to Wheeler's little office, and without delay was led by him to the great, galleried, underground room in which the finest antiques in the world were displayed.

It was truly a magnificent room, I thought, lighted with great amber clusters of tubes and by concealed lights behind the cornices and pillars. Some of the stands simply held cabinets of porcelain, pottery, silver, or glass, but others were fitted out as period rooms in which every piece was the best of its kind.

Wheeler explained that every day new goods were brought in to replace those that had been sold. Everything was carefully selected, examined by expert committees, and finally 'vetted' by himself. He said he had thrown quite a lot out that very morning.

Round the stands we went, and I was introduced to most of the 'big men.' They were very kind to me for my host's sake, opening cabinets, letting me handle their goods, and telling me prices. I examined the silver of How of Edinburgh, the china of Rochelle Thomas, and the oak furniture of Anderson of Welshpool. Of course, I bought nothing. I hardly expected to. But I thought to myself then, as I think now, that the success of such fairs meant that dealers would have to pay more for their goods, 'pull' provincial pieces to them, and so put up prices everywhere!

Wheeler was plainly exhausted, and no wonder. Sixteen hours a day, and the worry of the whole fair on his broad shoulders. He told me that despite the presence of several detectives (one of them carrying around a catalogue with his name and rank clearly written upon it until told to put it away quickly out of sight!) a jewelled gold snuff-box had already disappeared from a locked show-case in the very centre of the hall.

It was a crowded, bewildering day, but one thing stands out very clearly in my memory. Our lunch in the grill room! There was a huge Dover sole, with tartare sauce, and a coffee ice as big as a cricket ball, served with sweet sandwich biscuits and a silver tureen of whipped cream. I remember how the iced lager foamed as it was poured from a height into our tall glasses.

There are other fairs nowadays, and though they are no places at which to expect bargains they do enable the collector to see the very best of everything under one roof. He can meet more specialists in a few hours than he could visit in many months, perhaps years, of travel.

Of course, a possible alternative is to buy by post, a method which has this to be said in its favour—that pieces sent on approval can be carefully examined under the most favourable conditions, and returned if they do not satisfy, for it is well known that the only real test of whether one likes a piece is to live with it for a few days.

There are several dealers nowadays who do business entirely by post, but first to mind in this regard, in my own experience, comes William Pease who, as I have already mentioned, had a shop in Nottingham.

Tipping and I one day just before the last war persuaded our wives that we might be trusted to get off together for a week-end hunting trip, and off we set together in my car, to arrive in Derby late one Friday afternoon.

The commercial hotel we found in the London Road was very ordinary from the outside, but its charges were moderate. Not so its high tea! Con had begun to share out the biggest Dover sole I have ever seen, and a comparable bowl of chips, when similar helpings were placed before me. We slept well and breakfasted on sausage, bacon, and eggs.

We had hardly settled in the car when Con signalled me to pull up before a double-fronted shop. We got out. It was a very dirty shop, but clearly full of china of all kinds. We quickly spotted a few pieces we fancied, and decided to go in. A dirty, uncared-for shop does not always mean cheap prices, but you never know!

We tried the door, which was locked. We looked at each other and at our watches. Nine o'clock. We knocked loudly and waited. We were just about to leave when a door at the rear of the shop slowly opened, and an old, withered man peered at us over steel-rimmed spectacles. He was dirty, too, and bearded, and over his narrow shoulders hung some sort of coloured, patterned scarf.

He glared at us angrily, and his voice came thinly through the dusty glass.

'Go away! Go away! I will do no business on the Sabbath!'

Why is it that coveted pieces are so often out of reach in closed shops?

There was nothing else in Derby, and we decided to go on to Nottingham to see Pease, whom I had never met. We passed the county cricket ground, skirted the fine civic centre, and turned into Friar Lane, a steep and narrow street which climbs up the castle hill.

The shop had a single window, and led to the rest of the house by way of a steep little flight of stairs down which the dealer came to meet us, a short, slight man, elderly and rather bent, with a heavy moustache. He spoke in an unusually quiet, gentle voice.

When we had looked at the pieces in the shop we were taken into his sitting-room, and thence to a third room on the floor above. He had many fine pieces, including Derby figures, and much splendid pottery by Astbury, Whieldon, and Ralph Wood, but the only piece I can call clearly to mind was a particularly large Worcester tea-pot, blue-printed, and hideously 'clobbered' in red and gold.

Once more in his own room he opened a cupboard and took out a large photograph album, from which he selected a print of a pottery horseman. This he passed to us and told the following story:

'Ten years ago there used to be a little second-hand furniture shop just down this street. I used to call in now and again because they sometimes had a piece or two of china. Well one day I saw this little piece on top of a modern chest of drawers.

' "What's that?" I asked.

' "Oh, some sort of toy, I suppose," said the woman. "You won't be interested in that!"

' "Oh, I don't know," said I. "It's rather quaint. How much d'ye want for it?"

'And do you know what she said? "Tenpence ha'penny!"

'I bought it, and sold it for £250 a few days later. Astbury–Whieldon, of course, and a lovely piece!'

Isn't that the sort of experience of which every collector dreams?

Every piece sold by Pease bore a label—'Genuine Old Bow,' 'Genuine Old Longton Hall,' and so on. It was surprising that so many of them were correct, because even twenty years ago knowledge was nowhere near so advanced as it is today.

Both of us were made free of his code, each letter standing for a numeral in shillings or pounds. Every label carried both the cost and selling prices, and we were always allowed to buy at a figure somewhere between the two.

Nottingham was a fair distance from our homes, and for this reason Pease began to send us regular parcels of selected goods. As I write I have before me a letter from my friend in which he reports on a typical consignment. It is well worth quoting.

'I have a lovely parcel from Pease; it arrived a few days ago:

1. Sucrier and cover, Chinese procession with ox in it—unknown to us, this, with a large saucer dish to match. £5. Lovely, brilliant, and clean, with a lot of sapphire blue in it. I decided to have them.
2. "Blind Earl" dishlet, 2 tiny handles, "Chelsea" flowers. I decided to have that. £2.
3. Beautifully coloured floral Wall tea-pot, particularly sweet, £3. I decided on that also.

4. Tea-pot, see Bemrose plate 45, alleged Longton Hall. Poorly drawn, blobby Chinese decoration, 85 shillings. No. NO! I don't know Longton Hall at all well and thought to myself, "This pot might just as easily be called Liverpool."
5. Worcester juglet, floral decoration, nice, £2.
6. Ditto Bow, £2. Couldn't decide whether to have 5 and 6, a bit steep, but prices don't go down, and the £1 does! Later, heard from a good authority *re* the Longton Hall tea-pot! It's Liverpool, and worth 15 shillings at most! So THAT goes back, and I've asked for another parcel.'

Now this was in 1942, and I suppose any of these pieces could not be bought today for three times as much. Prices certainly do not 'go down'!

Like so many stalwarts of the golden days of collecting, Pease has passed on, but only a few months ago I found out, quite by accident, a very different side to his character. I happened to be in the home of a Derby friend, and I remarked upon a rather pretty flower painting which hung on his dining-room wall. It was well done, but clearly the work of an amateur.

As I looked at it my friend said: 'That's one of Pease's masterpieces! Did you know he painted? He asked me thirty bob for it, and having admired it I could hardly refuse!'

Five

THIS chapter is quite frankly something of a hotch-potch. An attempt, if you like, to recapture the memories of events, and feelings, and people that have all contributed their share to the making of a colourful score of collecting years.

How I wish, to begin with, that I could remember more of what was told to me by Owen Wheeler, that masterful, kindly figure who seems to keep popping up, willy-nilly, in every sort of connection. I can picture him so clearly, I can hear his cultured voice, and yet there is so much I cannot call to mind, not even all the stories, many of them related to collecting, but others having nothing whatever to do with it, which he drew from an inexhaustible fund.

There was an account of a fishing experience that occurred when he was stationed in Ireland, in salmon-fishing country, the tale of the tyro to whose line (when his back was turned) a great log was fixed, and of how he struggled with it in a raging spate for wellnigh half an hour, the while he shouted 'Fish! Fish!' to a heedless audience. The same man it was, so Wheeler said, who had promised gifts of salmon to numerous friends, and who was pardonably offended on hearing, years later, that it was my friend who had thoughtfully dispatched tins of salmon to those who would otherwise have waited in vain. Then there was the story of the youth who was unhappy because his tame canary turned out to be a cock bird and so could not lay an egg. Wheeler, seeing his distress, stole down at dead of night and placed a robin's egg in the cage, and next morning the house-party was wakened at an early hour by the youth's glad cries: 'Get up! Get up, everybody! Horace has laid an egg, after all!'

There was one story of a different kind. It appears that at a certain country house-party there was a particularly lovely girl who was unattached and who had done her best without very much success to captivate every bachelor in the house. They were all much too fond of fishing! However, one night Wheeler left the library after everyone else had retired. Everything was quiet as the grave. Now it so happened that the way to his room led past that of the lady, and he noticed that her door was ajar. He tip-toed past, but no sooner had he done so than he heard a very small voice, a whisper almost, 'Please, I think there's a mouse in my room!' He paused, knocked gently on the door and entered. The girl was lying on the bed and she smiled at him. What was more, she had prepared for bed without troubling to put on her nightdress!

'What on earth did you do?' I asked.

'Well,' said Wheeler, 'I was younger in those days!'

My wife and I spent a carefree fortnight with Owen on the Norfolk Broads, at a little place called Martham, in the blazing summer of 1938. He and his daughter, with her two children, were staying at a small farm, and he arranged that we should pitch our tent in a nearby field.

This was our first visit to East Anglia, but we broke our journey only at Norwich. Or, at least, we intended to do so because we hoped to see Wheeler's furniture at the museum. As it turned out we drove round in circles for at least half an hour until a kind policeman took pity on us and showed me how to get out of the town.

For a couple of days we quite enjoyed our camping. I slept on an inflatable mattress and my wife had a camp-bed. Each morning before breakfast, with the mist still lying low over the fields, I went in search of fish for breakfast. I saw a great many, but caught nothing. Tinned sausages were a poor substitute and gave me violent indigestion. What was more serious, my wife could not sleep on her camp-bed, and when on the third night it rained heavily that was the last straw. As she said, the rain might never come through, but how could one get to sleep when every moment one expected it would? So it was the farmhouse for us, and a big double brass bedstead. It was certainly more comfortable than the air-bed. Too little air in that contraption and the hard ground is one's portion; too much, and off one rolls on to it, anyway!

For the rest of our stay we fished and boated and yarned. In the evening Owen and I played chess, and I very occasionally won, when my reward was a handshake and a dissertation on the miseries of approaching senility. He slept badly and spent much of the night making innumerable cups of strong tea. He was always seated at his open window at break of day watching birds through his binoculars.

One day we went to Great Yarmouth to buy kippers. I once had an uncle who argued that if one aspirin relieved a headache, then a dozen would cure it that much more quickly. He applied the same principle with tomato fertilizer, but only once. He was wholesale, and so was Wheeler. The kippers came by the box, and I don't know which sickened us more, those or the bloater paste which he bought by the dozen jars. Bow-ties, suits, and shoes: it was always the same, and it was just as well that antiques were not so plentiful.

I can hear my readers asking, what has all this to do with collecting? And I confess I cannot answer. I know only that all the time, whether we fished or sailed, or merely talked, the bond was always there, just a little way in the background, always waiting to be expressed as we watched our floats or glided silently across some placid broad.

Owen found my wife a gullible subject for his love for leg-pulling. One rather misty day, warm and oppressive, we suddenly heard a distant booming sound echoing across the flat countryside at regular intervals of perhaps a minute or so.

'Did you hear that?' he asked, winking at me as he addressed her. 'You can tell anyone now that you've heard the booming of a bittern! Very rare bird, the bittern, and you are lucky to have heard it!'

She would hardly believe me when I explained later that lighthouse fog-horns do make a terrible noise on foggy days, any more than she would believe that a wall-eyed dog does not really use one eye to see by night and the other by day.

We had one day's hunting in Lowestoft, just the two of us, and in a little shop I bought a Worcester 'sparrow-beak' jug for 10s., decorated with alternate panels of flowers and gilt-marbled powder-blue. Wheeler found a part tea-set of what I would have called blue-painted Worcester, but which he claimed as Lowestoft. True to form, he distributed it piecemeal among several friends, with the result that I had a Lowestoft bowl, another had a 'Bow' tea-pot and sucrier, and a third gave cabinet space to a half-dozen 'Worcester' cups and saucers! It is a great thing to be an 'expert'!

We were just leaving when Owen spotted a large jug, ovoid in shape with a loop handle and a sharply-pointed spout, high up on top of a corner cupboard.

'What's that up there?' he asked.

'Chinese,' replied the proprietor. 'It's been up there for years, out of the way. No good to you.'

'Reach it down, and let me see it!' commanded Owen.

Down it was reached, with a deal of grumbling and panting. Then, of course, it was so dirty that it had to be cleaned. And only then was it possible to see that it certainly had a Chinese look, being decorated, every inch of it, with large mandarins and any amount of diaper pattern.

Owen handled it for a few moments, his head wagging a little, and his lips moving, as they always did when he was really interested.

'Hmph!' he grunted. 'Nice for flowers. Wrap it up. How much?'

'A quid to you, guv'nor!' said the man, and seemed surprised when Wheeler paid up silently and marched out with the newspaper parcel under his arm.

When we were some distance away, 'And what d'ye think I've bought?' asked Owen, a smile all over his face.

I thought hastily.

'A very nice Worcester jug, if you call it buying!' said I.

There and then he led me into a café, and over a cake and a pot of tea he explained at some length the possible virtues of the finest Liverpool porcelain, which at that time few but he had taken the trouble to identify.

Wheeler's first love was really fine porcelain, particularly the really good 'blue and white' of what he always called the 'KONG SHE' period. But as I have already said, he did understand old furniture, particularly oak, about which his book is still a classic. He invited me one day, while we were still on holiday, to go with him on a 'vetting' expedition, to see what was reputed to be a noteworthy Elizabethan buffet which had to be valued.

We entered a long room, at the far end of which stood the piece in question. I thought it was wonderful. What was my surprise, therefore, to hear Wheeler say, before he had hardly looked at it, 'I'm sorry to have to tell you, madam, that this piece is a reproduction.'

He went on to explain how this piece of carving and that chamfered panel bore the marks of tools which had not been invented at the time when the buffet was supposedly made, how this proportion was all wrong, and that joint out of keeping. Thus I learned that what is called 'flair' is not enough, but must be supported by a sound knowledge of timber, tools, and methods.

As we motored quietly home he told me more, and I remember vividly one story which concerned what he regarded as his most important 'find.'

On one of his buying expeditions he was told at a village inn that a certain baker owned a rather unusual four-poster bed, which he went to see. He recognized it as an Elizabethan piece with finely carved posts and head-board. The baker was willing to sell, and £10 changed hands.

Arrangements had been made for collection, and Wheeler was just on the point of leaving, when the baker said casually, 'That there piece came from the manor, you know. My old father bought it, and I've heard him say that there used to be some sort of a cupboard to match it. He didn't know where it went to, and I suppose it's been broken up long ago.'

Nothing more was said, but Wheeler had a talk with the landlord when he got back to the inn. He thanked him for his tip about the bed, and asked whether he knew what had happened to the rest of the furniture, or to any of it, when the estate was sold. The innkeeper scratched his head. 'Well, sir, I don't rightly know, for it was before my time. Half a minute, though, there's an old chap in the bar who might know summat about it.' He put his head through the hatch above the tap-room counter, and shouted loudly to an invisible 'George.'

George entered, and proved to be a very old man indeed, with a face like a withered apple, and completely bald. He was evidently very deaf, and stood there shuffling from one gaitered leg to the other, smiling and nodding first to the one and then to the other, as the innkeeper, prompted by Owen, put his questions.

Yes, he remembered the sale up at the manor, a little lad he was at the time. He didn't remember very much about it, but he did know as how a lot of stuff was bought up by the local folks. Old Hodgkins up at the home farm bought a mighty lot of things, but he was dead and gone, and the new man, Jones his name was, was getting things to rights in proper style, by all accounts.

That was all there was, shorn of a deal of irrelevant gossip, and Wheeler rewarded the old fellow with a pint.

Next morning he was at the farm soon after breakfast. As the old man had said, the new owner was evidently a man of action. The hedges were newly trimmed, the ditches deep and clear, and the old buildings were resplendent with new paint and gay patches of bright brown tiles.

At his knock the farmer himself came to the door, a young, strapping fellow, smart and businesslike, but affable and willing to talk. Yes, he had only taken over a few months ago and was getting things ship-shape bit by bit. And not before it needed it! You wouldn't believe the junk there was about. And the state of the land was a disgrace!

Wheeler let him go on, then took advantage of a pause to ask what had been done with the junk.

'Well, sir, old Smith, the rag-and-bone dealer, took several cart-loads, and the rest we piled up in the old barn there,' said Jones. Then he continued, 'Why, was there anything you're looking for?'

'Nothing in particular,' replied Wheeler, 'but I wondered whether there were any old corn measures, or wooden platters or anything like that?'

'You'd better come and see,' the farmer said, and led the way across the stockyard to a great barn, partly brick and partly timber, which they entered together. Its dim, sweet-smelling interior was pillared and raftered like a cathedral, and as their feet sank into a thick carpet of straw and chaff a cloud of dust arose to dance in the sunbeams which pierced the wooden walls, and a dozen hens left the hay which was piled roof high at one end to squawk protestingly past their legs and into the sunlight.

At least half the barn was filled with worn-out farm machinery, worm-eaten and rusty; ploughs, harrows, chaff-cutters, and so on. Wheeler picked his way carefully among them to where in one corner, behind a derelict threshing-machine, he could see a pile of old doors, planks, and posts leaning against the wall. With difficulty he pulled them away just for a few inches, and his heart leapt as he made out the outline of a large cupboard of some kind. It was too dark to make out any details, but when he thrust his arm into the gap his questing fingers felt some kind of carving. He turned round to face the farmer, who had not followed him, but stood somewhat impatiently in the open doorway.

'What's this behind here?' he asked.

'You mean that old cupboard?' was the answer. 'Damned if I know! We cleared it out of a pigsty. Why?'

'I'd like to have a look at it, if you think we could get it out.'

His companion frowned, and scratched his head.

'That's a tall order.' Then he said: 'But I'll tell you what. You come indoors with me for a glass of cider, and I'll get it brought out into the yard.'

He called to two men who were working in the stockyard, and when he had given them their instructions he led Wheeler into a large kitchen, where they sat down together.

Half an hour later one of the men poked his head round the door to say that the cupboard was out in the yard. Out went Wheeler and his farmer friend, and true enough there it stood on the cobbles. It was quite grey with dust and hen-droppings, its lower parts were in a sorry state with worm and dry-rot, and one of its two doors hung open and awry from the rusted remains of an iron hinge. It looked forlorn and out-of-place there in the sunshine, but Wheeler saw straightway that his search was at an end.

It was indeed the counterpart, as regards style, date, and carving, of the bed he had already bought, and the farmer was ready to sell it for £5.

A few weeks later, when both pieces had been carefully restored, they were sold for a four-figure price, because at that time fine oak was fetching high prices.

So, what with fishing, boating, evening chess, and collecting gossip, our Broads holiday came to an end all too soon. Con wrote to me shortly after our return home. 'I do rejoice you've had so happy and full a time, and look forward to details by and by. I'd have liked to be with you for a few days. G. O. is a great fellow, isn't he? As kind as the day is long.'

Whenever I pause to look at a certain side-table in my house I pick up a large, round platter which rests upon it, a piece of the rare Loughor delft from South Wales, heavily potted and crudely painted with a 'Chinese' landscape and with birds in green and aubergine. On the back is a label, bearing a number and the words 'Glaisher Collection.'

There is more than ordinary significance in that label, because this particular collection, as everyone knows, is housed in the Fitzwilliam Museum at Cambridge, and is, moreover, the subject of one of the most sumptuous two-volume catalogues ever published. Why, then, in my home have I a piece which apparently has been parted from its companions?

There is, of course, a reasonable explanation. I did not steal it! The fact is that Con knew a very famous South Coast dealer who was another of those 'characters' whom one is constantly meeting in the collecting world. In fact, very few of our friends were not characters, in one way or another, for like calls to like.

I met him only once, but I heard a great deal about him. I knew, for instance, that he possessed a certain watch which, so the story had it, had once belonged to his ancestor Oliver Cromwell. On the anniversary of the birthday of that famous man the watch was placed with ceremony in the centre of the dining-table, and all present rose to drink to the great Protector's memory.

I knew, too (and this was a strange thing), that certain paper-covered novels in the chain libraries bore his name, rather luridly sentimental tales of love in the tropics, well written, but certainly giving no clue in their contents as to his cultured, scholarly nature. Every year it was his habit to take a long ocean cruise during which one of these novels was written. Thus at one and the same time proper local colour was assured, and the expense of the holiday well covered.

To this dealer, then, came the opportunity of visiting the home of an old lady to whom Dr. Glaisher had bequeathed many of his finest pieces before the Fitzwilliam gifts. He went down to view, and in the course of time he was able to buy them all.

Now at the time when this happened very few collectors knew very much about old English pottery, and even fewer collected it. The result was that every few weeks Tipping received a parcel, the contents of which were picked over and bought by him and by a few of his discerning friends. Prices were naturally very low, and a mutual friend named Bruce George, in particular, very soon had a collection of pieces the nature of which was understood by few. I often admire, for instance, a very fine jug covered all over with that peculiar, intense pigment known as 'Littler's Blue.' It was known even then that William Littler used it on his Longton Hall porcelain, but it was not common knowledge that he used it upon his earlier earthenware. But Glaisher knew.

It is very true to say that many collectors, having gathered together porcelains of all kinds, turn at last, as their taste matures, to the simpler, unpretentious merits of old English pottery. When they do so they often have to suffer the ridicule of their fellows. Only a few years ago I was in Chester, and in one of the shops in the Rows I met a dealer who had known Glaisher very well.

'Oh, yes,' he said, 'I knew him well. In fact I found a great many of his pieces for him, and didn't I get my leg pulled by the other dealers!'

One of the classes of ware which Glaisher collected cheaply, in the face of much contradiction, was a family of pieces which he called 'christening baskets.' They were made of common reddish clay covered with lead glazes in brown, green, tan, orange, and gold, their sides pierced or ornamented with trelliswork, 'prunts,' flower-heads, leaves, and medallions, and with twisted, looped handles. Everyone said they were modern German, but he declared them to be medieval English of the thirteenth and fourteenth centuries. When Con bought those that came his way he set to work to confirm Glaisher's opinion, and published his reasoned, scholarly conclusion in the *Apollo* magazine.

It is a far cry from old English pottery to Chinese stone-ware and porcelain, but here again, quite by chance, we fell on our feet in the lovely little Cotswold town of Bourton-on-the-Water.

In those days the Windrush whispered under the many little stone bridges clear and undisturbed. Bourton was not then the miniature Blackpool or Hampstead Heath it has since become, and except on Bank Holidays one could admire its green lawns and golden houses in peace and quiet.

My first visit in company with Tipping was the occasion of my introduction to a dealer named Dawkes. At least, he had a little antique shop, though by training (at the Birmingham School of Art) and by inclination he was an artist and interior decorator. Many of the hotels and private houses in the neighbourhood have plaster ceilings colourfully decorated with his Tudor roses, portcullises, lions, and fleurs-de-lis.

When we had talked a while, and examined his small stock, we had tea together in a great barn, open to its heavily-timbered roof, and galleried at one end, that had been many things in its time, among others a chapel and a carpenter's workshop, but was now a tea-room. It is mentioned, in fact, by Priestley in his inimitable story of an English journey, and when we knew it, it was furnished with antiques of every description, and gay with enormous bowls of English garden flowers.

Among other pieces we admired were several pieces of old Chinese celadon ware, and when we expressed surprise that such things were to be found in a Cotswold village we were told that a lady in the district was selling piece by piece a considerable collection. Dawkes had hesitated to buy, for how many passers-by would know the first thing about Oriental art? Now, however, his appetite whetted, 'Get me some more!' said Con, and during the following weeks piece after piece came to hand. I remember a glorious shallow bowl or saucer-dish, covered with an intense violet glaze and incised with a pattern of dragons, and a great celadon bowl with a glaze like candle-fat that dripped down in globules from the foot-rim. But above all, the most important piece that came our way was a large T'ang horse and rider, that lived for some time most incongruously in a cabinet of 'blue and white,' simply because it was too tall to stand anywhere else!

That rather drab creature was a worry and a pest for some time. The question was, 'Is it right?' No one seemed to know. We certainly didn't. Our novelist friend, who knew a great deal about Chinese pottery, said he thought it was. Finally, in despair, we took it down to London, where Hobson of the British Museum needed but a single glance to give a favourable verdict. I think it passed on for £40, which I suppose was cheap.

The ending to many a venture into the mysteries of Chinese art is less fortunate. A single lifetime is by no means long enough to master them, for not only are the Chinese (and the Japanese too) expert beyond belief in reproducing the antique, but in addition they count it a virtue to do so, so great is their reverence of age in any shape or form.

The motor-car has revolutionized collecting, and the modern collector can cover considerable ground in his hunting during the course of a year. There is, however, at least one happy hunting ground that has always been readily accessible, at least until the outbreak of the last war. I refer to the legendary Caledonian Market.

I think my first visit was in 1935. I was told that I must visit this wonderful open-air market, where (so I was told also) every Friday morning London's thieves and fences congregated to dispose of their ill-gotten gains! I heard, too, of some legendary woman who had bought a shilling necklace of 'black beads' which turned out to be worth several thousands of pounds. Such stories, I knew, had to be taken with a grain of salt, but there was no harm in hoping, and my wife and I took the Underground at Marble Arch one autumn morning in time to alight at the Caledonian Road station just after eleven o'clock.

The market itself was perhaps a quarter of a mile square, surrounded by a high wall, and with several entrances. In the centre, as I remember, was a huddle of covered stalls or booths, surrounded by an outer ring of uncovered ones, the whole encircled by pitches which were merely spaces marked out on the cobbles. When we arrived some of the dealers were still engaged in arranging their goods, and we did as everyone else seemed to be doing, and hurried to the centre to spot the bargains, or so we hoped.

We were quickly disillusioned, for the booths appeared to be nothing more nor less than branches of Bond Street shops, which I suppose is what many of them actually were. The goods were of the highest quality, mostly fine silver and expensive porcelain, and never had we seen so many diamond rings and fur coats gathered together in one place! The uncovered stalls promised better things, and we stopped first to listen to a cockney dealer who held aloft one end of a large hearth-rug, made out of a black bear-skin with a tiger-skin worked into its centre. At the end of ten minutes' furious salesmanship, during which from time to time he shook the rug to prove that the hairs would not fall out, it changed hands for the astonishing sum of 18s.! No one seemed at all surprised.

We walked for miles on the damp cobbles, and had little to show for it. And yet, I suppose, if we had not at heart expected too much I should have been satisfied to buy an agate-ware pottery tankard in cream and brown clays for a shilling. That, and a Worcester small plate printed in blue with the 'pine-cone' pattern, for 10s., were our only purchases.

The outlying pitches on the ground had this in common with similar ones in any other open-air rag-market—how on earth did their owners make any sort of living? Some were piled high with dirty clothes and down-at-heel boots and shoes, others with tattered books and magazines, and every alternate one, it seemed, had as its stock-in-trade a miscellany of roller-skates, dumb-bells, rusty sewing machines, bits of machinery, and such-like. And yet every one was surrounded by a motley crowd of ill-clad, unwashed humanity, and every now and again a few coppers changed hands. I suppose nothing is really quite unsaleable, but the Caledonian Market stalls almost attempted the impossible.

I understand the market has been reopened, though on a smaller scale, but I have never visited it again. Somehow its atmosphere blends ill with a love of beautiful old things.

I have no doubt that London is still the place to buy antiques, though the war has brought many changes. I remember that twenty years ago almost every other shop in the King's Road, Chelsea, was either an antique gallery or a junk-shop, but where are they now? Where is the proprietor of that corner shop I visited one Saturday evening to come away with a clean and perfect Worcester bowl printed in puce enamel by Hancock, which I bought for 15s., and to leave behind a Pinxton cup and saucer, marked, and painted with a landscape, perhaps by Billingsley himself, because I thought it was 'too dear' at twice that sum? It was not so much a question, in those days, of finding good pieces, but rather of deciding how many one could afford to buy.

Kensington Church Street, winding its half-mile way from Notting Hill Gate down to the High Street, seems to change little. It must be the most interesting 'collecting street' in the world, and I was told by a dealer that there are still over fifty antique shops in a quarter-mile radius. I have never found them all, but I can well believe it. It is that sort of street.

At the very top of the scale there are several 'galleries' proper, whose window cabinets are filled with pieces that one might imagine ought to be hidden away in safes. They breathe an atmosphere of affluence, and of high prices, and are therefore positively forbidding. Next there are quite ordinary shops, most of them specializing in china and glass, with a few really expensive pieces arranged side-by-side with what are usually called 'dealers' goods.' Some of these may hold treasures, because their proprietors usually buy in lots for the sake of one or two pieces. Moreover, one is not so conscious of a thinly-lined pocket! Junk-shops proper are few, though there are plenty of tiny lock-ups (with even tinier cubby-holes of offices leading off) whose owners seem invariably to move in a very short time to larger premises, and to be able as a rule to take one down some back street to a cellar where most of the stock is kept. One may find, too, a kind of shop which seems to hold out possibilities which never materialize, shops which are lined with shelf upon shelf of large vases, bowls, and figures that look so attractive at a distance, but which turn out at a closer acquaintance to be hopelessly damaged or faked. The floors of such places are usually piled high with plates and dishes, none of which have any interest whatsoever, and to navigate which it is advisable to remove one's overcoat. Of general antique shops there are remarkably few—the emphasis is all on china—but here and there is a second-hand furniture dealer who cannot help but buy a piece or two of pottery or porcelain, if only to set off his chests and sideboards. In the window of such a one I once saw a large porcelain group, so filthy that had I not known its shape I should not have recognized it for what it was. I bought it as Bow for £12, but it was really a perfect Chelsea–Derby 'Neptune,' complete with his dolphin, most gloriously enamelled and, of course, a masterpiece of modelling.

One of the first London hunting-grounds I found was a short lane tucked away behind Selfridges, called St. Christopher's Place. It is really a miniature Church Street. Strangely enough, so many of its shops are all too often closed, and this always when some attractive piece attracts, maddening and tantalizing, from a dim corner. The consolation is, of course, that it is a fallacy to think that because a coveted piece is tucked away in a dowdy shop, surrounded on all sides by rubbish, it will necessarily be unidentified and therefore cheap. It seldom is!

Apart from the auction rooms, which I shall discuss later, there are endless possibilities in London. Wimbledon, Shepherd's Bush, Hammersmith, and so one might go on. Every suburb holds exciting possibilities, and if disappointment is all too often one's lot, is there not always the exercise?

Hearsay evidence is not acceptable in a court of law, and it should never be accepted by collectors!

Many years ago a friend told me glowing tales about a shop in Ross-on-Wye, in Herefordshire. He was not a collector, and he had not been inside. All he knew was that it was simply crammed with china of all kinds and that it was usually closed.

Off I went to Ross, and found that my friend's report was at least partly accurate. It was crammed with china, and certainly it was closed. In addition it was a very large shop, in the shape of a letter L on a corner, with, I think, six large windows. These were so dirty that it was difficult to see through them, but the china was piled high in show-cases against the walls, on tiers of open shelves, and on the floor. So far, so good. Now, how to get inside?

Next door was a grocer's shop, and an assistant directed me to a door between two shops on the opposite side of the road. That, he said, was where Mrs. So-and-so lived, and she would probably be in.

There was no bell, but there was a letter-box above which was fastened a rusty iron knocker. I looked through the slot, to see a long bare corridor ending in a straight staircase with a door at the top. I put my ear to the slot and could hear nothing. I knocked. Immediately there was a furious barking of some large dog, and a querulous female voice. The door at the top of the staircase opened, and a large, hairy creature almost as big as a small donkey descended like an avalanche, scrabbled along the corridor, and brought up with a terrific thump against the street door, still barking with all its might. I quickly withdrew my eye from the letter-box and prepared for flight.

Then followed a competition. The woman screeched alternately to her dog and to me, the dog raved and scratched furiously at the door, and I yelled my wants through the letter-box. Eventually I won, and the commotion inside subsided. The creature was hauled away and shut up, the woman emerged, and together we went into the shop.

As you will have expected, there was nothing there. The place had been combed time and time again by every dealer within twenty miles and more, and all that was left could fittingly be described as 'crockery.' On the other hand, just inside the door was a pair of arm-chairs which looked good, carved and gilt, and covered in tapestry. English or French? And whichever they were, were they cheap or dear at £25? I just did not know, and I realized that it is a mistake to study one branch of antiques to the exclusion of all others. One never knows what may turn up.

The woman saw that I was interested in her chairs, and asked if I would like to see what she had in the basement. Out of the shop we went, down a hill at the side, and through a short alley to the basement door. She entered first, and switched on a few pale electric lamps. The apartment was long and narrow, and as full of furniture as the shop above was full of crockery. There was just enough room to walk gingerly between tottering piles of chests, sideboards, cupboards, and chairs of every description, and every piece, so far as I could see, was full of worm.

I made my excuses, bought a Caughley blue and white printed dish to appease my conscience, and came away.

Of course every collector knows of such places. The explanation is usually, as it was here, that a dealer has filled his shop with goods at a time when antiques were given away. When he dies his widow or his daughter, knowing nothing of values or of provenance, is an easy victim to every crook who comes along, and she is quickly left with nothing but rubbish.

Six

THE long war years brought to every man and woman some personal, private grief, apart from the miseries of separation and bereavement that were a part of that terrible time. For myself, happy in my growing understanding of and love for pottery and porcelain, and in the birth of a son who I hoped might one day follow in my footsteps, I selfishly resented the end of my week-end jaunts and the partial interruption of my intimacy with Con Tipping. I resented these things, knowing that they were trivial in comparison with the wider issues, and the grief and desolation of those appalling years.

There is no point in a tale of this kind in dwelling on the havoc and the utter, lonely, hideous, stark ruin in so many cities and towns. When I went to London, as I still did from time to time, I was depressed and angered beyond words, and whatever I had read never prepared me for the piteousness, the extent, the futility, and the heartache of it all. It was comforting to return home to my few treasures.

So it was that my collecting was restricted to a rare day in the Cotswolds, usually by train or bus, and to that side of my hobby which can be pursued by the fireside—writing about one's possessions, and trying to pass on one's knowledge and happiness to others. And, of course, in order to write one must have something worth while to write about. In my own case I chose eighteenth-century English blue and white porcelain.

I described in an earlier chapter how I sold or exchanged my earlier pieces, but I did but touch upon my reasons for doing so. Briefly, I think it is not enough to collect any and every piece which by reason of its rarity or beauty makes an almost irresistible appeal, although it is true that a valuable and enviable collection can be made in that way. Only (and this is a personal opinion) it can never really satisfy.

I can hear someone say, 'But how about the Schreiber Collection in the Victoria and Albert Museum? Could there be anything more satisfying?' To which I reply, 'We are not all Lady Charlotte Schreibers; we have neither her purse nor her opportunities, and we must inevitably feel frustrated when we realize that, collect how we will, we can never reach a point when we can feel content to have reached our goal.'

The general collector may fill his home with beauty, but if he is one who makes a study of his collection he can never say, 'Search how I will, there is nothing more to find.' I am not saying, mark you, that anyone has ever been, or will be able to say it, but it is a good thing to hitch one's wagon to a star.

There is one other factor which influenced me, and which is well worth bearing in mind. There is usually something to covet in every good antique shop, but who nowadays can spend so widely? On the other hand, the specialist knows that his purchases will be fewer and at the same time more exciting.

I knew, of course, that 'blue and white' would be cheaper than polychrome wares, but my choice was influenced also by a very different factor. Because by early training and by nature I love beauty, my collection had to be of pieces which were at once lovely and workmanlike. The same paste, glaze, and potting are common to polychrome and to blue-painted and printed wares, but the latter are reticent and clean, they do not shout, and since only one colour was used the artist or engraver was obliged to concentrate upon good drawing and well-proportioned design.

Forty years ago blue and white porcelain, especially if marked with the Worcester crescent, fetched very high prices. Even a common printed tea-pot could be priced as high as £20. Fortunately (or unfortunately, whichever way you look at it) there are phases of popularity in antiques as in everything else and by 1939 it had slumped, so that I was able to buy cheaply. Strangely enough, high prices were still asked by small dealers in the back streets. I found often that a single ordinary piece in a dusty little shop was ridiculously priced.

'Ah!' the dealer would say. 'Ah! That is crescent-marked Worcester, a very rare piece indeed!' Whereas better specimens, many of them marked, could be seen by the score in a London gallery, properly priced.

I believe that when I sold my large collection years later I could have related the circumstances of the purchase of every single piece. Even now, when I browse through the pages of my first book, *English Blue and White Porcelain of the Eighteenth Century*, many of the illustrations recall them vividly to mind.

A Worcester cornucopia, featured in a coloured plate, reminds me of Miss Baker and her little shop at Quatford, near Bridgnorth in Shropshire. What a charming, sweet woman she was! The Severn never strays far away from the main road between Kidderminster and Shrewsbury, and her house commanded a lovely view of the valley. A pretty, perky little house, painted white, perched high by the roadside so that its cellar opened to the footpath, and one day as I was passing I noticed that the swinging top half of this cellar door was open. More, for outside on the path was a single antique oak chair, the window was clean, and inside I caught the gleam of copper and brass, and the sheen of china.

I parked my car down a lane a hundred yards away and walked back. On a chair inside the door was a handwritten notice, 'Please Ring, Loud,' and I pulled the piece of string which led to a bell hanging from the rafters. A few moments, and a woman descended the short flight of rickety wooden steps which led upwards into the house. As she came she pulled from her hands a pair of gardening gloves. I found very soon that Miss Baker loved her garden (that was why one had to ring loud!), and that she lived alone. She was the daughter of a country parson, a simple, scholarly soul I gathered, who had left her so poorly off that she kept the little shop to make ends meet.

Of this I knew nothing for some time. I saw nothing I wanted though everything was very underpriced. That was not my business, and I said nothing but just kept on calling.

Then one day she invited me up into the house, through a tiny kitchen, into Quality Street. Every white-painted cheerful room was filled with really lovely things: furniture, silver, pictures, china, and glass. A magnificent Chamberlain's Worcester tea-set filled the glazed cupboard of a Chippendale secretaire, Chelsea and Bow figures smiled coyly from a Sheraton cabinet, and on a little pie-crust table stood a fine Dresden group of a coach and horses. Everywhere there were great bowls and jugs of garden flowers.

That was the beginning of a much closer acquaintance. Many was the picnic lunch we ate together beneath an apple-tree on her little lawn, and many were the cuttings and roots which my wife brought home in triumph in the boot of the car. In return I helped her with her prices.

She was pitifully poor. She had a little Blue Persian cat, a dignified, elderly gentleman who loved her as she adored him. One day she said to me, 'You know, Mr. Fisher, I am afraid I shall have to have him put to sleep, for I cannot afford to keep him.' That was how close she had to budget. When he had toothache, and a vet. was called in to pull his teeth, I know she starved herself to pay the bill.

Every Saturday morning off she went on the bus to Shrewsbury, where the dealers put by anything cheap which might interest her. They stood on one side at the local sales and allowed her to pick up an occasional bargain, which had to be very cheap indeed, because she told me one day that her capital was never more than £20. She greeted me on one occasion with the news that she had spent everything on a single piece of old cut-glass, and asked if I thought the 10s. profit she asked was too much. It was always so difficult to persuade her that 6d. was not enough to put on an article which had cost her, say, 30s.

One evening, soon after I had arrived home from school, she rang me to report the lucky purchase of a pair of cornucopias, fluted, painted with flowers and insects in underglaze blue, and marked with crossed swords. She had bought them as Worcester, and she was dreadfully worried in case I thought she had paid too much.

'What did you pay?' I asked.

'Well, you see, the dealers made me pay more than I intended, but I thought of you and I'm afraid they cost £4. Can you come over soon and say what you think?'

I was with her in less than an hour. The pieces were indeed Worcester, in mint condition, and she would not think of letting me give her more than £6 for the pair. Even at that price she thought she was robbing me.

Two years ago I heard that she had died of a heart attack, probably brought on by her single-handed gardening. I have often wondered what happened to the little cat.

Many of my pieces were bought at auction, notably at Sothebys. I could not often attend their sales in person, but I pored over the catalogues and was able to picture most of the pieces described. Some were sold separately, but many lots comprised a dozen or even more, and these were very exciting. One could send a bid and await results! It was my practice to employ a London dealer to examine the lots and to send me a report, or to get a report and an estimated price from the auctioneers themselves. They would then bid for me, and I never found that there was any sort of attempt to raise the bidding, which is what one would expect from a firm of such high repute.

It might be supposed that this sort of buying would be uninteresting. Not a bit of it! A few days after sending my cheque along would come a packing case, and then the fun would start! First, layer upon layer of straw, then beautifully wrapped brown-paper parcels and, finally, each piece separately wrapped in tissue-paper. Even cracked pieces were treated in the same careful way.

This unpacking was naturally most exciting when I had secured a mixed lot. I remember one package which contained, or should have contained according to the catalogue, 'twelve pickle-trays.' They might have been anything, and their price was 30s.

I was delighted to find that I had bought two large Liverpool shell-dishes printed with the Worcester 'pine-cone' pattern by Zachariah Barnes, a pair of rare Longton Hall leaf-dishes painted in typical pale blue with Chinese landscapes, several dainty Lowestoft ivy-leaf pickle-trays, and four Worcester ones, all perfect. I should have paid at least £1 each for them in any shop.

Any country sale of the contents of a big house is bound to include a few lots of blue and white. I remember one very well because one of the lots comprised a dozen or so large 'Nankin' plates. Now that word can mean many things, from inferior export Chinese ware to blue-painted K'hang H'si or early English porcelain. Whatever they had been (and in fact they were export ware) I should not have bid for them, because they formed part of a frieze in the hall, and were very firmly fixed indeed. Nevertheless, they fetched a good price, and I wish I could have seen how their purchaser got them down!

In the library at the same sale was an oak overmantel with a very high shelf, upon which were several pieces of the kind I was collecting. No one appeared to be at all interested. They were well above the eye-level, and in any case were thick with dust. I found a chair and stood on it to investigate. Two Worcester rosewater ewers, bottle-shaped, three large jugs, a tea-pot, and a Dutch delft bowl with a piece missing. Several dealers used my chair when I got down. Still, when the lot came up they smiled at each other and left me to it, with the result that the only opposition came from a local lady who dropped out at £4 10s. At £5 I had a very good buy, and I restored the bowl, which made a good container for bulbs.

Another sale I attended was of the surplus pieces of a millionaire collector who had moved to Ireland. There are times when one would give anything to have a good bank balance, and this was one of them. In the so-called surplus there was the making of a good collection. The sale was so specialized that there were but twenty dealers present, and prices were very low. Among the pieces I bought was a very fine, lustrous Lowestoft coffee-pot decorated with landscape reserves on a powder-blue ground, which was good enough to be reproduced in colour in my book on blue and white, and which cost me £7.*

Among the dealers present was my friend of the Oriental peach-shaped wine-pot. He would never have any dealings with the 'Ring,' and there he sat like a Chinese image at the end of the

---

* It has since changed ownership several times, appearing twice at Sothebys, where it was last sold for nearly £200.

long table, glaring at them and daring them to do their worst. Up came a Chelsea plate, one of a set of twelve to be sold separately.

Without hesitation, even before the auctioneer could speak, 'Twelve pounds!' said he, defiantly.

They were all so stunned that the hammer came down without another bid.

What is more, he got the other eleven for a few pounds apiece. He knew his values, and he had customers for that kind of ware, whereas the other dealers were not so fortunate.

When one specializes the time soon comes when it is an occasion to find a new pattern, and it is then that the high-class dealer in porcelain has to be patronized. It is terrifying almost to enter a shop whose great windows contain pieces of Chelsea, Bow, Worcester, Meissen, or Sèvres priced in hundreds of pounds when one's own resources extend, perhaps, to a ten-pound note. On the other hand, it is better to buy one fine piece than to spend a pound here and a few shillings there on odd cups and saucers.

One day when I was in London I paused before one of the two windows of a Bond Street gallery famous for its fine porcelain, for in the very centre, on a stand all to itself, stood a large Longton Hall ewer-shaped jug, moulded, its scrolled panels covered with brilliant, smudgy 'Littler's Blue.' It was not priced. It was very lovely.

I gazed longingly and passed on. This I did several times, for I could not tear myself away. At last I plucked up my courage and walked in.

A young gentleman in immaculate morning dress asked my pleasure. Could I see the jug in the window, please? By all means, and in a moment I held it in my hands. At least, I thought, it would be something to have handled it!

On the sides were faint traces of the unfired 'size gilding,' and to my delight (and dismay, for surely it would put the price up) under the flat base I found the almost legendary mark of the crossed L's.

At length, 'What is the price?' I asked.

'Twenty-five pounds,' said the salesman, and went on to tell me all those things I already knew.

I thought to myself, that was not too bad! I had expected a figure twice as much in Bond Street. I calculated hastily. Luckily I had my return ticket home! On the other hand, I had never paid anything like that for any piece in my collection. What would my wife say?

I said I thought the price was too high, and made to walk out.

But no! My friend was made of sterner stuff. Perhaps they might 'put it in' a little cheaper if I was interested. He would call our Mr. So-and-so, and off he went to return immediately with another gentleman even more resplendent, with gold in his teeth and diamonds on his fingers.

Was I interested? Was I a collector? And so on. Until, finally, a very lowest price of £18, and the jug was mine. I have never bought another piece in London's most exclusive and expensive street, but it sold at Sothebys some years later for £45.

Every collector does a little swapping when opportunity offers. Thus a fine Lowestoft bowl decorated in powder-blue came my way in exchange for a Chelsea–Derby covered custard-cup painted with flowers. Whenever Con bought blue and white I had the first chance to buy it, and sometimes a friend, knowing nothing about china, would risk a few shillings on my behalf. One such brought a pair of little cream-jugs, for which he had paid £5, but as they were Liverpool, painted nicely with flowers and with 'biting snake' handles, no harm was done. My mother was not so fortunate when she presented me with a pair of Japanese covered vases which cost her £1. They still stand on my mantelpiece, but they were not 'the kind of stuff I know you like'!

I shall have something to say later about the arrangement, cataloguing, and photographing of a collection, because they are labours of love. For the moment, however, it is enough to say that, all these things having been done, the idea of writing about my blue and white became so compelling that in 1944 the purchase of a little mug set me going in earnest.

I had often passed by a certain local second-hand furniture shop without troubling to go inside, but one particular Saturday morning, in a show-case at the side of the window, I noticed a nice flask in pink and white Nailsea glass. (I bought it for £1, and it shot out of my hand like an orange-pip when I washed it in soapy water!) I went in, and the dealer told me that it was one of a few pieces he had found in his cellar, all of which he had bought many years before. He had the rest in a back room, and showed them to me.

I forget the other pieces, but the one which intrigued me was a small mug made, I thought, at Caughley. It was decorated with eight little identical Chinese water-scenes, each labelled 'COBALT,' and a letter, a different one to each, in eight different tones of underglaze blue. On the bottom was the inscription '22nd May, 1787.' He was asking 15s. for it, and I took it home in my pocket.

Then followed a lot of research and a visit to Mr. Dyson Perrins, the famous authority on Worcester porcelain. He agreed with me that it was undoubtedly a trial piece made at the Caughley factory in order to try out different pigments, possibly for submission to Humphrey Chamberlain who at that time was decorating white Caughley ware at his Worcester studios. I persuaded a friend to photograph it in several positions with his Leica, wrote a reasoned article about it, and sent it to the editor of *The Antique Collector*.

To my amazement he accepted it—my first published article. Clearly, I decided, if there was that much interest in blue and white, now was the time to get started on a book about it.

Nothing has ever given me greater pleasure than writing about that collection. At the same time, though I was fairly sure of my ground from the technical point of view, I was very grateful for any help I could get to make the text clear and lucid and, above all, stylish.

The name of George Hamilton Ashe is well known to entomologists, but the man himself is loved by many hundreds who benefited by his skill as a teacher. I have already mentioned that he taught me how to draw, and when I began my book I was glad that he had also put me in the way of learning to write. An essay a week was the rule, on subjects as out-of-the-way as 'The Shape of Eggs and Why,' 'Mass Production,' 'Cheese,' and so on. His pupils had to be able to write about anything under the sun.

My next mentor was an inspector of schools, who kindly agreed to read the manuscript of a book I was preparing for school use. One warm summer afternoon we sat together in deck-chairs, and he turned the typewritten pages until he came to one paragraph in particular which he read aloud. Then he said: 'Tell me in your own words, just what did you mean to convey in that paragraph?' I told him. 'I see,' said he, 'and does that paragraph really mean just that?' I had to confess that it did not. That was a very valuable lesson in the choice of phrases and words.

At about the same time when I was preparing the 'trial mug' article I wrote another about an interesting Liverpool tea- or punch-pot, the manuscript of which I sent to Tipping for his opinion. This is what he replied:

'It isn't impulsiveness you suffer from; you're so often right. It's haste. I'm thinking of the reputation I want to see you with in ten years' time, say. You are right to offer suggestions and suggest possibilities in your writing, of course, but it must not be made up wholly of such. Any ordinary hack else could do what you and I will soon be specializing in. In time, you'll find, suggestion and possibility harden into facts, and facts make, in relationship, knowledge. Knowledge is always worth winning and always "saleable."'

With such advice in mind I set to work. Every chapter was first written in pencil and then typed late at night because my wife could not stand the clatter of the old Oliver which I had bought for £4 10s. and which I had learned to operate at speed with two numb fingers. This took six months, and I sent the results to Tipping.

A week later back it came, with his pencilled notes in the margins. My facts were not criticized nor, I was pleased to know, my clarity of expression! Still, since he was a master of the English language, which I certainly was not, there were enough suggestions to warrant yet another rewriting and typing.

The next step was to prepare the photographs, and here I was lucky. Or at least I thought I was lucky at the time, though as things turned out perhaps I was wrong.

I heard about an old retired bank manager who had a camera for sale, and I went to see him, with the result that I bought an old but perfect Sanderson quarter-plate complete with wooden tripod and assorted apparatus for £7. From what I saw of his photograph album I knew I should have only myself to blame for poor results.

I took photographs of all my best pieces against a black cloth, using a pale yellow filter to emphasize the blue decoration. I was quite pleased with the results, and the next step was to think about a publisher.

I know now how very lucky I was not only in my first choice but also in its outcome. I chose Batsford because of the high quality of their work, and off went my typescript and photographs by registered post. A few days later (and this was in the January of 1945) I had a nice letter from Mr. Hanneford Smith. They liked my work, but would like to submit it to 'an acknowledged authority.'

Now this was a poser! What did they mean? A writer, perhaps, or a dealer? I wrote back and pointed out that there was such a thing as 'professional jealousy.' The reply was reassuring. I need not fear that my work would receive any but fair treatment.

I sweated for three months. Then one morning I saw the postmark I had been waiting for. I hardly dared open the envelope, and when I did my wife looked over my shoulder.

All was well! I read that Mr. Bernard Rackham, no less, had reported favourably and that Batsford had decided to publish. More, for that great authority had agreed to write a foreword.

I lost no time in writing to Con, and I treasure the words he wrote in reply:

> 'I have had a specially happy day today, chiefly because of the lovely good news. I know just how you feel and can live again my own early experiences and thrills at getting into print on such a scale. Well done, indeed. Well done. It is most gratifying and exciting. Even I hardly know what to say first, for congratulation and pride and good wishes and bravos are so mixed in my mind and heart that it is hard to keep cool and reasonable.

'Your own judgement has been right all through. Yours was the inspiration, entirely, your own brain planned and executed. Your own tenacious industry saw the job through. You are never at all to reckon as in any way real the little service or two I did you. All I did was to clear away a little mist in your early manuscript, when there might well have been a great cloud. Well done, Stan. I mean it. The arch of attainment is superbly keystoned by Rackham. That he should do the foreword stamps the book with authenticity, reliability, and class.'

It was July 1946 before I received specimens of type-setting, and the suggestion that the whole batch of photographs ought to be redone! So much for my Sanderson, or more probably for my lack of skill in using it. It was not long before two professionals arrived with a van-load of expensive apparatus that included an enormous whole-plate studio camera with a lens as big as a pint pot, and a battery of floodlights. They took immense pains. The fact that my house is Georgian and solidly built did not prevent a request that a typewriter should not be used in the room above that in which they were working, lest its vibration should shake the camera! The result, of course, was perfect photographs. My pieces looked like porcelain.

When they left they took with them half a dozen pieces which had to be taken in colour under proper studio conditions, for we were determined that the tone of blue in each should be exactly right.

At last, early in 1947, I received my first proofs. That was a red-letter day, especially as I was told that a copy of them was to be submitted to Queen Mary in the hope that she might be graciously pleased to accept the dedication. A few weeks more, and on the same day I had Rackham's foreword and Her Majesty's acceptance of the dedication.

In October I experienced the happiest moment in any writer's life, the receipt of a parcel containing the author's copies of his first book.

'Dear Mr. Stanley Fisher,' wrote Mr. Hanneford Smith, 'at long last your *magnum opus* is ready for publication. I have much pleasure in dispatching to you today four copies, which please accept with my compliments.'

Of course, never before had there been such lovely books. We admired the binding, the paper, and the printing. We even loved the fresh, inky smell. We set the four copies on the table and gloated over them, and every now and then we would pick one up to find some fresh beauty or to read in print some paragraph which read so much better than it had done in manuscript.

I went to bed that night a happy man, but not before I had sent a copy to Tipping, the instigator and inspirer of it all. Before me as I write I have his letter, which I can never read without recapturing for a spell some measure of that first flood of rapture.

'My Dear Stan,

'There is ripeness in the air and heart this golden day, and I write immediately to thank and to congratulate you, and Muriel, and your father and mother, and the so far heedless youngsters, on the beautiful blossoming of your particular and private tree of knowledge. Well, it leaves me rather speechless, the arrival of this long-awaited day that was to bring me your book. You are proud to have found so becomingly handsome a vehicle for your thoughts, reflections, and labours in which even Batsfords have added to their reputation for beautiful books. I admire and like it without reserve: the colour plates are superb, and, more, exact to their intention. The print is clear and stately, the monochrome among the best ever: the whole presentation admirable and lovely indeed. Of your own careful and loving labours this is not the place to speak: you will have a surfeit of praise and commendation. Let it be enough that you show genius in order and method of presentation: you have been honest and not ashamed to admit "I don't know," you have created a harmony out of what has long passed almost unregarded and jungle-like. You have pioneered.

'For your words to me I cannot express sufficient gratitude: indeed our mutual regard one for the other has led you into a too generous appraisal of my influence and help as it might lead me into over-praising your careful industry and literary ability. Let us agree we'll sidestep all this and share one another's knowledge and joys, and especially our love of these frail and lovely things down, as Stevenson called it, "to the dusty gates of death." '

These were the words of a friend who, despite his expressed caution, was all too apt to use the superlative. Still, I was pleased with my *English Blue and White Porcelain of the Eighteenth Century*, and without exception the reviews were not discouraging.

I have very enjoyable memories of the great houses I have visited in order to advise upon or to write about collections of china. The first time this happened was during the war. I was asked to go to Chastleton House, near Stow-on-the-Wold, there to identify the china.

I turned off the main road a few miles out of Chipping Norton, to ask my way a few miles on of an old rustic who was trimming a hedge. 'Oh, ah! You're wanting the Great House,' said he, and a great house it turned out to be, a tall, almost menacing pile of greyish-buff wall pierced with staring, mullioned windows, and flanked by two square, battlemented towers at either end. A strong, gaunt, unyielding place, yet peaceful in the warm morning sunlight, cradled between church and stables in lofty elms and spreading oaks.

Mrs. Whitmore Jones met me at the door, and led me straightway through a pillared screen into the panelled Great Hall. She paused before one of the many pictures of her ancestors, a wonderfully living portrait of an early seventeenth-century lady, upon whose little finger the artist had painted a large ring.

My guide pointed to her own hand. 'See,' she said, 'I am wearing it now upon my own.'

That was a foretaste of living history that was continued throughout the house, in the furnishings that had grown up with it, in the very scent of three hundred unbroken years of gracious living. From the hall we entered the White Parlour, so called because its arcaded panelling was painted in Queen Anne's time, furnished with Jacobean walnut chairs and tables, and brightened, for me, by the presence upon a table of a complete tea-service of

Nankin blue and white porcelain. Then into the great dining-room with its lovely moulded plaster ceiling and with one long wall entirely covered by a magnificent Lille tapestry, up to the Great Chamber on the floor above.

This is one of those rare apartments in which the utmost skill of craftsmen in many trades was lavished without regard for cost or time. I looked at the cunningly carved panelling with its colourful frieze of panels of sybils and prophets, and thence my eyes travelled upwards to the geometrically planned ceiling with its great pendant icicles. To my right, as I entered, I saw the massive stone fireplace, its severity relieved, colourfully, by a great painted coat-of-arms.

Finally, when we had traversed many corridors and peeped into many a room hardly less splendid, my guide took me into the Long Gallery. How wise were the architects of former years to create such havens of peace at the very top of their great houses! The panelling was superb, the arched, wagon ceiling, decorated with roses and fleurs-de-lis, something to marvel at, but it was the peace, the utter silence of the place that so delighted me. Mrs. Whitmore Jones may have guessed at my feelings, for she left me there to sit in an arm-chair in the sunlight, content for a while to absorb, if I might, some of the atmosphere. Here, I thought, if anywhere, there must be happy ghosts.

That day, I remember, I had a frightful cold, and while I was content to admire I was very loath to work. At length I returned to the Great Hall, where great Chinese bowls and delft platters lay on refectory tables, and on these I began by placing in each a small card upon which I pencilled attribution and date. This I did right through the house. There were many services, of course. In particular, an amazing set of Staffordshire white salt glaze, moulded in silver shapes, alternated according to season, on the dining table, with a coloured service of Spode. In a cabinet in the dining-room was set out a Flight, Barr and Flight service bearing the family arms, gaudy, perhaps a little ostentatious, but a marvel of the china-painter's art. In a corridor I wondered at a perfect set of Jacobite glass made, it is said, by Hartshorne himself, and at a seventeenth-century glass posset-pot which was the finest I had ever seen. Even in the disused kitchens there was treasure, for here was pewter of all kinds, shining as brightly as silver though no longer in use.

Before I left my hostess took me outside to see the four great stone pillars, in a little vault, which support the main staircase. I looked up at the guttering far above my head.

'What a very tall house this is!' I exclaimed.

'Yes, I know it is almost exactly 80 feet in height, because that is the length of the ladder which was made especially to reach the roof. Come and see it.'

Mrs. Whitmore Jones took me to a long shed, and there it was, its sides made of one great slender tree split down its exact centre. I cannot guess how heavy it was, but I was assured that four men could with difficulty raise it into position.

Such was Chastleton, and such, I suppose, it still is. The collector is happy indeed who can feast his eyes upon such treasures. I left with reluctance as the rooks were cawing home to their nests in the tall elms. Within a few months I returned, for I had been invited to go when I wished, to see more at greater leisure.

Unfortunately some American visitors arrived as I did, and there was no one to show them round, the lady of the house being otherwise engaged.

Then 'I wonder, would you mind showing these ladies and gentlemen round the house?' she said to me.

What could I say? For all I knew they might well know more about its contents than I myself! I fear I spoke a deal of rubbish, but I enjoyed my task, and if they suspected my knowledge at least they did not give me away.

Seven

ONE day just before the end of the war I heard about the private collection of a man named Harry Lewis, which according to my informant included 'sumptuous Swansea pictures on Derby porcelain, gloriously rich Chamberlain, a great deal of Whieldon, a grand 5-inch wine-bottle of Dwight's stoneware, some fine Astbury jugs, and a large collection of air- and cotton-twist wineglasses.' This was a list which indicated that here was a man of catholic taste, and I lost no time in persuading Con Tipping, who knew him well, to introduce us.

Every room in a largish house had its cabinets of porcelain, every mantelpiece its burden of figures or vases, but it was the pottery that really took my eye, for that was superb. I quickly found that Lewis was not a lover of what might be called the dry bones of collecting. He paid little attention to factory history or to the technical perplexities of potting, pastes, and glazes. Above all, he loved beauty and could afford to pay for it. The result was a most varied and interesting collection, and I doubt whether I could have named any well-known kind of ware of which he did not possess a good example. His was the kind of collection, in fact, that makes the specialist doubt the wisdom of his choice.

Most of the collection proper, apart from purely decorative pieces, was in the library, but upstairs, in a little room whose walls were lined with open shelves, I was shown literally hundreds of pieces of domestic ware, mostly plates, jugs, bowls, and tea-pots, all of earthenware of some kind, which comprised in effect a history of the Potteries.

So you see here, in one house, was a collection displayed in two ways. On the one hand part of it was purely decorative, to be admired by anyone, and on the other there was this little room where the enlightened could browse and study. I think every collector would wish to imitate such an admirable arrangement.

Among so many hundreds of interesting pieces first impressions cannot be very distinct, but among those that particularly attracted was a set of three porcelain jugs of the same design but of different size. They were unmarked, but undoubtedly Chamberlain's Worcester, and each was decorated in bright colours with two Rowlandson *Dr. Syntax* subjects. It did not take me long to decide that they were faithful copies of the prints in the 1812 edition of *The Tour of Dr. Syntax in Search of the Picturesque*, and I wrote an article for *Apollo* in which I linked up the book and the porcelain. In so doing I found that the same eccentric doctor had been represented also as a Staffordshire figure. I did not know, then, that Lewis had one, but sure enough, tucked away in a corner, there it was. Time and time again one finds this sort of relationship between different mediums in art, apart from that inseparable from such a cult as 'Chinese Chippendale' which influenced furniture, silver, ceramics, fabrics, wall-paper, and even architecture. Let me give another example.

Some years ago I found in a dealer's shop in Burford a large, well-carved wooden group of a centaur carrying off a not too reluctant lady. The sight of it rang a bell! Where had I seen something like it? I thought for a while, and suddenly I had it. Off I went to Cheltenham (having asked that the group might be properly photographed on my behalf), to see Bruce George, and to examine again a 19-inch group in white earthenware. Sure enough, it was the same subject. What was more, the pose was almost identical.

This group, I decided, was modelled by Enoch Wood, but still I knew nothing about its significance until only a week or so later I saw, in an old copy of the *Connoisseur*, an illustrated advertisement of a large ivory plaque, modelled in low relief, from the McAndrew collection. The subject was the same, and it represented the classical story of Nessus and Deïaneira.

There, then, was a kinship between wood, earthenware, and ivory, and I have no doubt that somewhere there is a bronze group, or a picture, which was the inspiration of the three pieces I had seen.

I have mentioned Bruce George several times, and it is high time that I said something about the most enthusiastic and (dare I say it?) 'cranky' collector it has been my good fortune to meet.

Whenever I stayed with Tipping I was always left to my own devices, every Saturday evening, while he visited Captain Bruce George. Always he took in his pocket a few of his recent finds, and usually he came back with something else. Only, for years I could never, never persuade him to take me with him.

'No,' he would say, 'he's a queer stick and he doesn't like strangers. One day, perhaps.'

Well, at last that day came, when a month or two after the war I was told that George would like to meet 'the lad.'

Off we went along the London Road until we came to a large house built in what might almost be called the Gothic style, lying back from the road at the end of a rather overgrown garden. He rang the bell, and without waiting for a response in we went.

Of a most amazing conglomeration of antiques of all kinds I will not for the moment speak. I had eyes at first for nothing but the man himself. Tall, thin almost to emaciation, bluntly outspoken, and a law unto himself in all that he thought or did. Many considered him to be eccentric or downright impossible, but no man shrewder, and certainly none more generous. I had been in the house little more than a minute when he picked up a little Enoch Wood figure of a naked-looking lion that I had admired.

'Put it in your pocket and take it home,' he commanded.

I demurred. After all, it was a good little piece. He straightway held it aloft in one thin, sinewy hand.

'Either you take it, or I smash it!' said he. 'Which is it to be?' I took it.

Mrs. Bruce George ran the house with the aid of an unreliable daily help, but an army of servants could not possibly have kept it tidy. Every foot of wall-space in the corridors and on the staircase was covered with old maps by Speed or Morden, Alken or Pollard sporting prints, Bartolozzis, oil-paintings, and steel-engravings. A visitor strange to the vast drawing-room would have needed a guide-book or a map, almost, to have found his way between occasional tables littered with bric-à-brac, past cabinets full of pottery and porcelain and crowned with enormous vases, to the great show-case, full of Staffordshire cottages, in the far corner. In the dining-room a wealth of silver was displayed on a small Hepplewhite sideboard.

The most amazing room was Bruce George's own study, in which there was just room enough to sit down after chairs had been cleared of books and magazines. One side was completely filled by a big show-case whose glazed upper doors reached to the ceiling, so filled that I do not believe a single other piece could have been crammed in. As I found out later, the cupboards beneath were scarcely less crowded, but were seldom opened because so much other furniture, and so many of the larger pieces of pottery that cluttered the floor had to be moved in order to get at them at all. Figures, vases, and every other sort of china were placed haphazardly upon every ledge and shelf of the ornate sideboard and carved overmantel, and the table defied description. Among other things that jostled with more pieces of pottery and porcelain I noticed a typewriter, a tray in which stood a bottle of sherry, a wooden tray full of correspondence, and a large instrument something like an antiquated phonograph the use of which I have never discovered to this day.

That visit was the first of many, and I never knew what would be spread out on the table for me to see. Every local sale and every Saturday morning hunt contributed its quota of interesting pieces. One day I found two enormous, ugly, carved Chinese images leering at me from the hearth-rug, as fat and as big as barrels.

'What on earth are those?' I asked.

'God knows!' was the reply, 'but they'll look well in the garden. You can have 'em for a sovereign; I don't want 'em.'

Neither did I. Nothing more was said, and in complete contrast he passed across a box which I opened to find a perfectly delightful, dainty ornament of carved jade, a large chaplet or wreath cunningly designed in the likeness of lotus-blossoms and foliage. No sooner examined and admired than a shift to a Whieldon figure, and thence to a late eighteenth-century coloured print of children by Hamilton, in its original black, gold-starred glass mount.

Like old soldiers, true collectors never die. Or, at least, they never stop collecting. When, like my old friend, they are brought to their beds, the sale catalogues are brought to them. There they gloat over every description, and thence their orders are given to their wives who are fond enough to attend the sales. The pride of possession, whether it be for a lifetime or for a few months, is truly a wonderfully powerful thing.

With the war over my wife and I looked for a larger house, which at length we discovered in the shape of a Georgian mansion, almost, in the old High Street of Baldwin's Bewdley. In fact, it is only a few houses removed from his birthplace. We went to see it before it was de-requisitioned, and we knew that it had been occupied in turn by the Free French (as a hospital), the British, and the Americans. We knew also that it had been built about 1780 by an old Quaker named Samuel Skey, who was not only the town's banker, but also probably the richest merchant in the neighbourhood.

We opened the massive front door to enter what ought to have been the hall, but instead we saw before us a long, dark passage which ended, apparently, in a sheet of pale green glass, through which the daylight filtered dimly. Upon closer acquaintance, however, this proved to be a glass-panelled door leading out upon a little landing at the top of the stone staircase which curved down to the garden, upon which nettles had grown to a height of over 6 feet! The same family of giant nettles had, indeed, invaded the entire two acres of walled-in ground, for the military had been forbidden the use of it.

We retraced our steps along the arched corridor to find that the hall had been boarded in to form the sergeants' mess. That, we decided, was an apt name, because in the centre of the oak floor was a pile of ashes, empty tins, and other rubbish some 4 feet high.

Still, the matchboarding had protected the charming little stone staircase which led up into what had once been Skey's dining-room. This magnificent room appealed to us at once. In measurement about 30 feet by 20 feet, it was lofty in proportion with a good moulded plaster frieze, with, again, an oak floor. At the street end two tall sash windows, and at the other, overlooking the garden, a fine, pillared Palladian window in mahogany which it was said had been removed from Cannons, the demolished seat of the Chandos family. We decided—for I think we had already made up our minds to take the place—that this would be the drawing-room.

Down again to the hall, and back along the corridor, to find a makeshift kitchen that had probably been the servants' hall, from which rickety wooden steps led down into the damp gloom of the enormous coal-cellar, boiler-house, and laundry. My wife approved of the large pantry, a later addition with a rusty corrugated iron roof but facing east as was right and proper. Further along the passage, still on the left, we found a little gem of a room that had been the banker's counting-house. It had many delightful features. Of course, Skey had traded up and down the Severn in many West Indian goods, and he did not skimp the mahogany. This lovely timber covered the walls to a height of over 3 feet—one panel stretched the full 16-foot length of the room—and the small but perfect fireplace, in the Adam style, showed off its mellowed, golden beauty to perfection. But what attracted me immediately was the end of the room facing the big bow-window overlooking the garden. At one side was a panelled mahogany door, 2 inches thick like all the doors in the house, that did but hide an ideal arrangement of shelves and tiers of little drawers. The rest of the wall was built in with bookshelves above cupboards. I had never envisaged anything more suitable in which to keep my books, and yet another room was earmarked on the spot.

On the other side of the corridor we found a dining-room overlooking the street, and at the back, level with what I already called my study, we hoped to find our living-room. We opened the door.

Then—

'What on earth is that?' exclaimed my wife in a horrified voice.

Well might she exclaim! From the whole of the ceiling, which we could see was finely plastered, some sort of green fungus hung down to a depth of several inches. We stayed only to look out at the garden, and returned back along the passage, leaving the door open behind us to let the room dry out.

This possible home of ours was built on a plan very popular in the late eighteenth century, in that the main staircase mounted from a little side-hall leading off from the passage. It climbed in six wide, low-rising flights round a square well right up to the third storey, lighted by a narrow window from top to bottom. The treads and risers were of oak, but the carved balusters and gracefully curving rail, and the deep panelling on the inside, were polished mahogany. The owner of the place had already told us that he had been offered £1,000 for the staircase alone, and I could well believe it.

The bedrooms were in keeping with the downstairs rooms. One, in particular, we were surprised to find had a mahogany floor, as well as a stately and perfect William Kent fireplace in the same wood. Even the attics, though approached by treacherously low doors, and with exposed rafters, were large and spacious.

Now, on the top floor there were two landings, the one we had crossed, and another from which the back staircase led down into the darkness, guarded by a slender iron balustrade. It was spiral in form, panelled in deal, and winding round a central newel which, we were told, had once been a mast, perhaps from one of Skey's great Severn trows. We knew, too, that it led down to the kitchen, and so left it at that and descended once more by the way we had come. Only, this time, we did not stop at the ground floor, but continued on down the same oak treads, and past the same fine panelling, down to the basement. Here we found no less than seven rooms, including a wine cellar which still retained a few of its bins, and a meat cellar. What pleased me most was the fact that I should be able to fix up a dark room for my photography, as well as a workshop.

One last thing had to be done. The cellars. And to enter them we had to go outside, down the winding stone steps to garden level.

During the war they had been used as one of the town's principal air-raid shelters, and they were fitted with electric light. I noticed, too, that the arched brick ceilings had been reinforced with massive concrete rafters and struts. But above all their extent was most impressive. Two long cellars stretched away into the gloom to the street 25 yards away, and from one of them led another, and much older cave (for it was hewn out of the solid rock, and bricked only on one side), which had a large opening in the brick wall. This was a mysterious, oppressive place, silent as the grave but for a monotonous drip, drip, drip from the stalactites which hung from the lofty roof. But what was the hole in the wall? I remembered that I had a torch in my car, and I hurried out to fetch it. By its light I saw that the hole opened into the side of a deep well, apparently dry, and that directly opposite another opening, arched, stretched away into the darkness! Later we were told that this was the entrance to a passage leading to the church some 300 yards away. We like to imagine old Samuel Skey indulging in a little smuggling as a profitable side-line, but the more probable truth is that we have part of the old town sewers on our premises. How many secret passages have an equally prosaic explanation?

I must beg forgiveness if I seem to have dwelt over-long on something that might seem to have little in common with the subject of this book. And yet, to my mind at any rate, there is a connection. A collector is bound to be a lover of anything old, and what could better epitomize antiquity than an old and beautiful house? At the least, it is a fitting home for his treasures. Besides, I love the place. It is one of those houses that has a happy atmosphere. It greets you kindly, sweetly, as you enter, and bids you cast aside all depression. We are quite sure that old Skey loved it, too.

The wife of the owner, who had lived there for many happy years, is a Quaker, hard-headed, practical, and not given to foolish imaginings. She told me of a very strange experience. One sunny afternoon her children were in the garden and she was in the house alone. Happening to want something from a bedroom on the top floor she mounted the staircase, and was about to reach the first landing when before her, not 6 feet away, she saw a shadowy, yet perfectly distinct figure of a man in knee-breeches and cocked hat. She paused, and for a moment thought that what she saw was a shadow made by the sun, shining perhaps through the staircase window. But then, she decided, the sun was not yet round to that side of the house. Determined, though inwardly a little fearful, she went on her way, and as she passed the figure, whatever it was, so the outline changed, as it would if one walked round a living person. She stressed this fact to me, as being extremely important. A few minutes later, when she descended, there was nothing there.

I like to think that the old merchant may sometimes visit his old home. I have never seen him though I have often stood in the silence and wished that he might appear. If he ever does I know that his intentions will be kindly.

How many people have ever seen a milk-white mule? We know that Skey bred them, and that his delight was to harness a lively team to his town carriage. I believe he still does, for on more than one occasion, in the dead of night, we have been roused by the clattering of hoofs along our narrow street. At first, 'I wonder whose horses those are that have got loose?' we used to say. Or, next morning, 'Did you hear those horses last night?' All very ordinary and commonplace. But why, when one hurries to the window to look out, does the sound suddenly stop? And why, although the street is perfectly straight, is it always empty?

We took the house, and for several years collecting went by the board as we scraped, and cleaned, and polished to bring it back to life. When the painters had left then in came the electricians. No sooner had they gone than it was the turn of the plumbers and the heating engineers. And each, in turn, left behind still more mess to clear up, until we almost despaired of ever getting a proper shine to our lovely oak and mahogany.

The deal lining of the back staircase had been painted in an abominable shade of green, and this had to be scraped off. One day, when I came home for tea, my wife greeted me in a state of great excitement.

'Come quickly!' she cried, 'we've found a picture behind the staircase. I'm sure it must be a good one, because it's a portrait of a man in some kind of foreign dress!'

I hurried with her half-way up the spiral stair, and sure enough, by the light of a torch through one of the cracks between the boards, I too could see a little patch of some kind of coloured silk or brocade on an inner wall some 2 or 3 feet away.

Before I left the next morning I gave instructions that the workmen who were doing the scraping should remove one or two boards in order to remove whatever it was we had seen. I thought of all the things it might be. I even decided what we might do with the money it would fetch.

Of course, such things happen only in dreams, even to collectors. When I reached home (and I lost no time about it), my wife had a long face. 'Come and see the picture,' she said, and led me into the kitchen.

There, propped against the wall, was a sheet of tin, upon which was painted the portrait of a fiercely moustached, bearded gentleman in Eastern dress. Beneath, printed in large letters, was the legend 'RAJAH CIGARS, TWOPENCE EACH.'

I have often wondered how it got there. And why.

If I had to stop collecting china, at least I thoroughly enjoyed the adventure of furnishing our new home. Why, I wonder, do so many newly-weds rush to buy modern plywood furniture when gracious antique pieces can be found, with time and patience, at so little extra cost? It was decided, of course, that my blue and white should live in the drawing-room. I already had five cabinets, but they were full to overflowing, and I had to find another. Here I had a stroke of luck.

I forget how long ago it was when the contents of Marie Corelli's Stratford-on-Avon home were sold, though I do remember that there was unexpected competition for her gondola. At any rate, a few weeks after the sale I saw another of her possessions in the home of a Birmingham surgeon-collector, a great, bow-fronted mahogany cabinet, at least 8 feet in height. He had caused it to be properly fitted with electric light. Just what I'm looking for, I thought.

Shortly afterwards I saw it again in a Derby dealer's shop. Yes, I was told, sure enough it was the same one. The price was £45. I wanted the cabinet, and the dealer fancied a mahogany bureau in my possession. Accordingly, we did a level exchange there and then.

A few days later the carriers brought it to my door, and then the fun began. The two men were finally persuaded that it was possible to haul 4 hundredweights of glass and mahogany up eight stone steps into my drawing-room, but I hardly dared breathe until the piece was safely in position between the two street windows. The only thing I did not like about it was that it was lined with green silk brocade, but I found that just as black-basalt Wedgwood looks well against a yellow background, so does blue and white against green, if it is the right green. There is nothing much wrong with a bluebell!

The next thing I found was a carpet, a lovely Caucasian one over 20 feet long in glowing reds and blues that just suited the drawing-room. I found it in a local shop for £75. Unfortunately, not only was it so lovely that we dared hardly tread upon it, but it did not really blend with the china, and we sold it at a handsome profit to a London dealer and bought a blue Axminster instead. Then came a massive Steinway concert grand, much too big for any ordinary room, and a Sheraton cabinet on stand. This was where I made a bad mistake. There was nothing wrong with the top half, but the stand was 'made up,' as I found when I looked underneath. It had once been quite a nice little table, with graceful, tapering legs, and its underside was inlaid with squares of satinwood and ebony, evidently for chess.

One advantage of furnishing large rooms is that large pieces can often be bought very cheaply. Our drawing-room fireplace was enormous, and cried aloud for a tall looking-glass. This we found very quickly, an overmantel some 6 feet high, its large central mirror divided from the narrower, flanking ones by twisted pillars, with a scrolled cornice above, all beautifully gilded, for £2.

Certain kinds of mirrors usually fetch low prices at sales. I managed to buy two of the typical wide, mantelpiece mirrors with architectural columns and capitals, and with rows of little balls beneath the moulded cornices, for less than a pound apiece. One of them had a well-modelled gesso ornament, above the central glass, in the form of a Roman chariot.

What kind of pictures should one buy for a Georgian house? I chose, first, Bartolozzi and Cypriani prints, either in sepia or in colours, partly because they have such dainty round or oval gilt frames. They were a glut on the market only a few years ago, but they are coming into fashion again, and prices are going up. Silk pictures, too, and here again I think their attraction lies to a great extent in the way in which they were originally framed. I refer, of course, to the fact that the glass was painted black on the inside, relieved by a narrow gold border and by a gold star or medallion in each corner. Only a silk picture is not worth buying if there is any damage to the delicately painted faces of the figures.

Twenty years ago there was a vogue for glass pictures, which are comparatively rare nowadays because they are so very fragile. Nevertheless, they are extremely decorative if they can be bought in good condition. The process of manufacture was to glue a good engraving to a thin sheet of glass, after which the paper was soaked off until only the black ink remained. Colour was then applied in washes. A genuine example can be easily recognized by its thin glass, often disfigured with little streaks and bubbles, and by the apparently haphazard blotches of raw colour on the inside. I say genuine, because imitations have been made by gluing ordinary coloured prints to the back of modern window glass.

Nothing is more decorative, or more suitable for the walls or an old house, than coloured county maps by Saxton, Speed, or Morden, in that order of date. They look best in narrow black and gold 'Hogarth' frames, and examples that have printing on their backs, usually referring to towns and villages, ought to have glass at both back and front. We bought several nice examples, but here I am afraid I cheated. You see, uncoloured maps can be bought for a tenth of the price of coloured ones, and if one's aim is simply to decorate one's home, and not to make a profit by resale, what is easier than to do one's own colouring with water-colour or crayon?

Oil-paintings sometimes tend to take the lightness from a Georgian room, but one day, at a sale which included many fine pieces from the former Worcestershire seat of the Duke of Bourbon, one of the lots was a large oil-painting of a woodland scene, over 4 feet wide, in a dirty but massive gilt frame. I liked the warm greens and browns, and I liked the subject. It was knocked down to me for 15s. Fortunately, my car had a sunshine roof, and I got my purchase home by crouching most uncomfortably under the half that projected over my head.

When I had cleaned the painting with 'Germoline' (which is good for pictures as well as for cut fingers) I decided that the scene was set in the Wyre Forest, a misty glade among oaks and elms, with grazing deer, and several rabbits scuttling around a burrow in the foreground. In the left-hand corner was the artist's signature, but I could not make it out, neither could Mr. Seaby of the Birmingham Art Gallery, who came down to look at my find. Whoever he may have been, he achieved a rather remarkable effect, because, dependent upon lighting and upon the time of day, no one can ever decide whether he worked in the early morning, in the full blaze of noon, or at sunset.

Our own living-room, we decided, had to be furnished in oak, which is better able to withstand the rampaging of two small boys. Here my old friend Braithwaite turned up trumps. For as long as I had known him much of his china had been displayed on the shelves and in the cupboards of an enormous oak dresser, over 6 feet long, with graceful cabriole legs, and nicely inlaid with a darker fruit-wood. Whenever I asked him if he was ready to sell, 'What would I do with my china?' he would say. At last, now that I could show that I had real need of it, he consented to sell. At the same time he found for me a large corner cupboard with similar inlay, a large oval drop-leaf table with bobbin-twist legs, and (because I had missed the wonderful chest-on-stand with the enamelled plaques) a plainer, gentlemanly piece with the fronts of each of its five rows of drawers carved in a different geometrical pattern.

I thought that with all these pieces nicely arranged we could pass on to mahogany, but no! My wife said she must have a bureau for her private papers. And bureaux, even oak ones, cost money.

'Why not go to Price's?' she suggested, and off I went to see the dealer from whom I had bought the big mirror.

He had one bureau, to be sure, and its price was £6. It looked dear at the price. One bracket foot was missing, the runners had gone from every drawer, the sloping front had lost its hinges, and some vandal had removed its original brass furniture in favour of wooden knobs. Nevertheless, I bought it.

It took little time to effect the necessary repairs, and I was able to buy a new set of reproduction handles and escutcheons. Only one thing then spoiled the appearance of our new piece—the gaping, irregular hole that served for a keyhole in the falling front. I designed what I thought was a typical keyplate of the period, found a piece of thick sheet brass, and cut and filed it to shape. It is now the nicest feature of the bureau, but I should not like to make another.

There is all the world of difference, of course, between furniture made by a cabinet-maker and the thousands of pieces made by village carpenters. This particular bureau seems to possess the characteristics of both. On the one hand, the drawer fronts and falling front are properly veneered, while on the other hand the corners of the carcase are quite crudely dovetailed, with no attempt to hide the joints. How fascinating it would be if one had a history of every piece in one's possession!

I remember that when I bought the bureau the dealer showed me a pair of mahogany buckets or pails, with vertical slats, bound with brass hoops and with brass handles. Down the side of each was a slot about 2 inches wide.

'Do you know what these are?' he asked.

I said I had no idea, but what had he paid for them?

'I can sell 'em to you for a pound apiece,' he replied, and I bought them, for whatever their purpose they were handsome, perfect pieces.

A few months later, when I had rashly sold them at a small profit, I saw an illustrated advertisement in a collectors' journal of one of my buckets, or at least of one exactly the same. It was a plate bucket! I might have guessed. Our Georgian ancestors had so many labour-saving devices despite their rambling houses. I had made a bad mistake, and here was yet another proof that a collector simply cannot afford not to learn as much as he can about everything he sees. Knowledge always pays rich dividends.

It would take a very large book to describe in detail the furnishing of a sizeable house, and it would probably be boring reading. Let it suffice to say that at last we thought the house was passably accoutred, and we had now to give some thought to a sadly depleted bank balance.

I decided to sell my collection.

Of course, knowing how much I loved my blue and white, my wife objected.

'Why not sell part of it?' she suggested.

Now I thought at the time, and I still think, that such a course is always unwise. The gaps would bring back so many memories. In addition, and perhaps more important, so long as a few pieces remain in the cabinet there will always be the urge to add to them. No! I decided it must be a clean sweep or nothing, and the sad business began of packing my pieces into tea-chests, ready to be taken down to Sothebys by road. You may be sure that I lingered long over many a one of them.

It was very strange, when I received a copy of the sale catalogue, to read the descriptions of my own pieces, and it was admittedly annoying to find pieces that I remembered so well losing all identity in lots which were made up of as many as two dozen pieces. Someone else, for a change, would take advantage of a 'lucky dip'! In the end I did well, for all but one or two of my reserves were exceeded. Financially I was in pocket, but I could not bear to enter the room where my cabinets stood so empty and forlorn.

No wonder that we collectors are looked on as cranks! We scour the countryside for rare pieces, we bring them together to form a harmonious whole. And then, having gone to all that trouble, we separate them so that someone else may begin all over again!

One of the last interesting experiences I had before my collection was sold was the giving of a short broadcast. I forget now how it all came about, but I do know that I arrived at the Birmingham studio of the B.B.C. at eight o'clock one April evening. The place was an old school, dowdy and typically Victorian, but the inside was a hive of feverish activity. My talk was to be part of a weekly feature called 'Midlands Miscellany,' and its title was 'The Story of Blue and White.'

The producer, Cedric Johnson, took me straightway into a tiny cubicle in which were two chairs, a table on which was a microphone and a reading-desk, and a large clock with a prominent second-hand. There we began to rehearse.

I always wondered just how every B.B.C. programme manages to finish just on the dot. I soon found out. Three times did I read through my script, until at length it had been pruned and re-pruned sufficiently to allow me to finish just as the second-hand crept round to zero.

At ten o'clock sharp Johnson and I sat again in our box. He gave me my last instructions. I was not to rustle my script, not to cough, and to be ready to begin as soon as he had introduced me. Oh! And one other thing! The red light meant SILENCE!

I was the second of three speakers, and I was surprised to find that the other two were in London. A namesake, James Fisher, came to the close of his talk on 'John Clare, Poet of Nature' (of which I did not hear a word though his voice was blaring from a loud-speaker not a foot from my ear), Johnson introduced me, and I was 'on the air.'

I have never wanted to cough so much in all my life. I was absolutely terrified lest I should make a slip. Sweating, I managed to forget the microphone and all the millions of listeners, and to read steadily through the words I knew almost by heart. Thanks to our rehearsal I finished dead on time.

When I arrived home an hour later I had a pleasure in store. A friend had recorded my talk on his tape-recorder, and I sat down to listen to my own voice for the very first time. Of course, I had the shock of my life. Was my voice really so high-pitched as all that? Was that really me, that careful, pedantic teacher's voice that betrayed all too clearly my country origin? Still, there was, perhaps, just a trace of culture? No? Ah, well. At least I did not stutter.

It occurs to me, such is familiarity, that in my description of my own home I have been so preoccupied that I have made no mention at all, so far, of a much more interesting house that stands but a stone's-throw distant from it. Tickenhill Manor was well known to the first Elizabeth, and it was the scene of the marriage by proxy of the young Prince Arthur, but of its ancient splendour and impressive size nothing now remains but the massively timbered remnants of the Great Hall, around which the existing Georgian mansion was built. Many collectors who are interested in the lives of our grandparents know it well, for Mr. and Mrs. J. F. Parker had devoted many years of loving service to the making of a museum of bygones. It is a good thing, in these hurly-burly days of modern progress and mechanization, to be able to examine at leisure the kind of things men used to make with their hands. Here, for instance, was a wheelwright's shop, and here a pewterer's. Here, salvaged from a nearby town, was a reconstruction of a druggist's bow-fronted premises, and room after room was filled with early bicycles, perambulators, vacuum cleaners, typewriters, kitchen utensils, and sewing machines. There was a fascinating collection of children's toys and books, and old costumes beyond count. And yet, only here and there was it possible to find anything that might fittingly find a place in a Bond Street gallery, although paradoxically there was a great deal that one might hope to find in that Mecca of all collectors, the attic or the lumber-room. The truth is that most folks' cast-offs were Mr. Parker's treasures, and let there ever be a country sale, or the rumour of an impending one, and off he went on his bicycle, on the bus, or on the train, to return triumphantly in due course, weary, but happy in the knowledge that posterity is the richer for his labours.

One day we set out together to a big local sale, for there were some things he coveted that were considered too good to be given away. Among them, in the stable-yard, was a certain pewter chamber-pot, of unusually small size. Parker explained to me that in Georgian times, when the ladies had left the gentlemen to drink their port, it was convenient to keep such utensils hidden away in small cupboards in the sideboards. He had such a sideboard, but lacked the contents.

'I must have that pot!' he said to me. 'If I bid for it someone will smell a rat, but if you act for me you'll probably get it for a few shillings. Remember, I simply must get it!'

'That's all very well,' I objected, 'but supposing someone else does want it? How high will you go?'

'They won't, but I'll pay five pounds if necessary!' he said.

The lot was put up, amid a great deal of chaff and laughter. To make matters worse it now included two more pots of cheap earthenware, one of them lacking its handle.

'What am I bid for these useful articles?' asked the auctioneer.

'Five bob!' I shouted, and of course every eye was turned in my direction. I was about to turn away to hide my blushes, but not a bit of it! Across the yard a very pretty young woman, her face even redder than mine, but plainly determined, raised her voice. 'Ten shillings!' she said.

'Ten bob I am bid for the jerries! Any advance on ten bob?' said he with the hammer, and the battle was joined. We might have been bidding for a Titian at Christies, judging by the excitement, and each of us soon had partisans egging us on with advice which, though certainly useful, was not always in the best of taste. My opponent was quite undaunted, however, and in less time than it takes to tell the bidding had risen to £5, against me. I glanced across at Parker, who nodded. 'Guineas!' I said. No reply from the opposition, and that was that. I joined Parker, who was smiling ruefully, and no sooner had I done so than the young lady came across to where we stood, accompanied by a rather horsy-looking man. 'I'm so sorry about that lot,' she said. 'I didn't really want it, but my husband bet me five pounds that I wouldn't do my best to get it, and now I'm afraid it has cost you rather a lot of money!'

So it had, and Parker was right, after all, in his valuation!

I may have given the impression that during several years of furniture-buying I gave up looking for china. Actually, apart from my own reasons for visiting antique shops, I was always on the look-out for pieces for my friends, and even made many new friendships.

One dealer whom I will not name really traded in modern china and glassware, but he was always willing to sell old pieces on commission. Unfortunately, he also bought a piece or two for resale, and since his knowledge was extremely limited every collector for miles around almost lived on his doorstep. His practice was to try to keep a likely piece until everyone had seen it and to form his own opinion (and fix a price) according to the decision of the majority. It seemed to work out very nicely.

I was told that he had a very comfortable house in the country which had been bought in a most peculiar way. It appears that a gentleman brought in several rather fine Oriental vases which he wished our friend to sell for him. The price he asked was £100.

Now there are very few collectors of really expensive Chinese porcelain, and the pieces stood neglected on a shelf, gathering the dust, for several weeks. Not even the weekly Saturday morning local 'boys' showed any interest. Then one day, in walked a rich collector who happened to be staying overnight in a nearby hotel. He saw the vases, and to cut a long story short he bought them for a very high price indeed.

When the owner came to pick up his money he was, of course, told of this wonderful stroke of good fortune, when to my friend's amazement he refused to take any more than the sum he had suggested. I never heard how much more was the price that had been actually paid, but I do know that it was more than enough to buy the house!

It is a good thing to buy for friends provided their wants (and the depth of their purses) are known. I like nothing better than that they should do the same for me. It is a friendly act, and from a purely selfish point of view one has the pleasure of examining and learning unaccustomed things. For example, I knew little about gilt furniture until an auctioneer friend decided to buy it, and asked me to remember him on my travels. This he did after he had admired and bought a pair of gilt brackets, supported by lions' heads, that I had bought in a junk-shop for half a crown and put out of sight in my cellar! Without his request I would never have dared to buy, for myself, a pair of mirror-sconces, Venetian I suppose, from a Wallingford dealer, or another pair of brackets of carved wood in Shrewsbury. He was glad to have them, and I learned by handling them for a few days.

Buying for dealers is quite another matter. One dealer I knew very well was always asking me to buy this or that for him. One day it was Bristol delft, another it was wrought-iron gates, and on this particular occasion it was 'Canton' enamelled porcelain. Sure enough, I happened to find such a piece, a largish mug with a twisted loop handle, richly enamelled with flowers and Chinese figures, for 30s. I took it with me the next time I went to see him.

'Was this what you asked me to find for you?' I asked.

'Hm! Decoration a bit sparse, isn't it? Not really what I wanted. How much did you give for it? Not too much, I hope!'

'Thirty-five bob,' said I.

'Much too dear!' he almost shouted. 'I can pick 'em up any-where for half a sovereign. No good to me at that price!'

It took me, I should think, a quarter of an hour to sell that piece for what I had given. I was determined he should not get the better of me. And if I had any doubts at all as to whether I was justified, they were removed when I called in again a week later. On the mug, too dear at 30s., was his label, and on the label, in his code, was the price—£3 10s. 0d.!

Some there are who make a living out of what I tried to do just that once. The most thick-skinned man I have ever met was a certain Turkish gentleman who traded on the fact that certain kinds of antiques are dearer in one part of the country than in another. I have met him in many dealers' shops, with his little Gladstone bag from which he would produce a pair of plates, a silver coaster, or a bit of Battersea enamel. This he would plank down on the counter, and until he had sold it he was quite impervious to insults, threats, and rebuffs. Sometimes, instead of cash, he would take goods, and I am perfectly sure he was never the loser.

Every collector of experience knows that he sees the same pieces time and time again in different parts of the country. I once bought a figure of Justice in a Black Country shop for 18s. It was sold to me as Bow, it was actually Chelsea Derby, and its head had been broken off and very carelessly glued on again. That is why it was so cheap. I sent it to London, where the head was properly restored, so skilfully that only I, who knew it had been off, could just make out the new joint. I sold it for £5, declaring the damage, and within a year I saw it again in Gloucester priced at £15, and in Birmingham at £25. Some day, when the pink enamel round the neck has faded to yellow, it will be sold again at a rock-bottom price.

No one will ever fully understand the mystery of antique values. A local dealer buys a piece at a small sale, and within a few days in comes a London dealer who buys it from him at a trade price. Then, some time later, a provincial dealer visits London on a buying trip, and back comes the same piece, at a still higher price, into the very neighbourhood whence it was first taken! Finally, of course, a collector pays the limit.

What with one thing and another Con Tipping had never found an opportunity to visit my new house, but in the autumn of 1949 he came to spend a week-end with us. I fetched him over on the Friday evening, and the following day we set off into the Black Country. There is little to tell, for not until we passed through Birmingham on our way home did he manage to buy a clean Leeds tea-pot painted with flowers and pink net diaper, and a stately coffee-pot of the same cream-ware. I found nothing at all.

The next day, the Sunday, was sunny and warm for the time of the year, and we sat out in the garden after dinner, yarning, and sitting silently for minutes at a time in that comradeship which does not call for speech, until it was time for me to take him home.

I forget why I had to hurry home, but since I had arranged to see Harry Lewis on the following Tuesday evening I agreed that I should call in for a night-cap on my way back to Worcestershire. They lived only a mile or so apart.

Con accompanied me to the door, holding in his hand the piece we had just been discussing, a little piece of wood-carving from some church or other, representing the 'Pelican in her Piety.' He laid it down on a table as we reached the door, and shook my hand in both his own, as he always did.

'Thanks, Stan,' he said, 'for my pleasant visit. I'm glad to see you and Muriel and the boys so comfortably settled. I feel all the better for it. Good-bye until Tuesday. Good-bye, son.'

He stood on the pavement, and as I turned the corner I looked back, and we waved to each other.

I was finishing my tea on the Tuesday when the telephone bell rang. I answered it. It was Harry Lewis, and of course I thought immediately that he was about to tell me that he could not see me as arranged.

'I felt I must ring because I knew you were coming here and thought you might call in first at Con's,' he said.

Then—

'I don't know how to tell you, but our dear friend died late last night of a heart attack.'

I cannot tell how long I stood there with the telephone in my hand. There are some things one cannot immediately grasp. I could hear Lewis's breathing at the other end of the line, but he said nothing.

At last—

'Do you mean Con?' I asked.

'Yes,' he replied.

I managed to thank him, I think. I do not know what I said.

For the next few days I walked and went about my business in a daze of misery. I could not speak about him to anyone. Even to think about him brought the tears to my eyes.

On the day of the cremation I went down to his home. I could not speak to his wife and daughter. We just stood, looking at each other. I went to sit in my usual chair in the study, his own empty one close to my right hand. The afternoon sun streamed in through the open window and struck little diamonds of light from the hearing aid which lay on the top of his roll-top desk. And as I sat I tried very hard to reach out, somewhere, to where he was, and I spoke what was in my heart that he might hear.

At the service in our college chapel the Principal, later the Dean of Worcester, spoke eloquently in his praise. And all the time, as I sat with my eyes fixed on the coffin that was trestled a few yards away before me in the aisle, my brain was shouting, 'O, Con, my dear, dear Con, they don't know one half of it!'

I watched while the bearers carried him away from my sight into the sunlight of the green quadrangle, past the 'sunlight in stone' of the buildings he loved so well, but I did not go to the cremation itself. I felt I no longer had any part in anything that had to do with him. I drove slowly home along the Tewkesbury road, and only then, I think, did I realize that I should never see him again.

Con's death ended a chapter in my collecting life. It had always been so easy, and such a delightful thing, to seek his advice, always so joyous a thing to be able to share the pride in a new possession with one who understood. Above all, perhaps, I had been so pleased to think that he might be a little proud to know that his teaching was beginning to bear a little fruit.

'Just you wait for a year or two, my son, until I have retired! There's such a lot we shall be able to do together.'

That was what he so often said, but now I was on my own, and I felt that there would be little savour in anything I might do.

Owen Wheeler, himself an ailing man whom Con and I had not expected to outlast the previous winter, wrote a short letter; he was too heart-broken to say very much, but he ended—'D'Artagnan has gone to the Happy Hunting Grounds, beloved by all who knew him. May his dear soul rest in peace.'

There must inevitably be a strong bond between the master and the disciple, but I am glad to think that our affection for each other was that of father and son. That apart, Conrad Hinton Tipping combined learning and humility to an uncommon degree. Essentially he was a countryman with a deep and abiding love for his Gloucestershire hills and for everything English, a love which showed itself, too, in an unbounded tolerance towards human failings. His friends knew he would never let them down, and they were ever confident that his vast knowledge and unerring wisdom was always at their disposal, however busy he might be. His enthusiasm was infectious and limitless, and his gifts as a teacher enabled him to pass on to others the fruits of his scholarship, some of his unfailing instinct for truth, and his cold logical reasoning, whether by the spoken or the written word.

Sometimes, when the house is quiet at night, I try to convince myself that he is near, ready and willing to advise me in that quiet, serious voice of his. I try to believe that my decision on whatever is troubling me, whatever it may be, is not wholly my own. And when I tried to explain to Wheeler, several years later, that I could sometimes feel, almost, that our old friend was not very far away, he said, 'My boy, if you believe that with all your heart, I am quite sure that he is.'

Eight

THERE is no better investment than good antiques. Certain things have their ups and downs, both as regards popularity and price, but the trend of values is always upwards, and bargains must be rarer year by year. I turn over the pages of a priced sale catalogue of about ten years ago. True, I see few 'snips,' but the prices are ridiculously low by present-day standards. Here are some of them, taken as they come.

Flight's chocolate cups and saucers, 'Japan' wheatsheaf style, and a tea-pot in the same style. Another Barr period chocolate cup and saucer, and another of the Wall period	£19
Wall period *famille rose* bowl painted with flowers on a dark blue ground, a saucer-dish, 3 cups, a coffee-cup, 3 saucers, square and W marks	£28
4 Wall period coloured baskets, 6¾ inches, painted inside with flowers	£42
Wall period oval basket, painted with flowers reserved on dark blue ground, with pink and green buds at the intersections	£26
Pair of Wall period scale-blue plates painted with exotic birds, 7½ inches, crescent marks	£28
Pair of Wall period dessert dishes in Sèvres style, painted with birds against a landscape background, rich blue border, and 3 plates, 7½ inches, with the same decoration	£80

Pair of Wall period scale-blue cabbage-leaf jugs with mask spouts, painted with flowers, 7½ inches, square marks £42

Chamberlain's Worcester jug, 8¾ inches, inscribed in gold with 'Success to the Coalbrookdale Iron Works, J. H. 1800,' 'Japan' style decorated on a coral ground. Chamberlain's inkstand with a view of Waterloo Church, 2½ inches, and 3 mugs painted with views of Malvern and Worcester £18

Flight, Barr, and Barr Worcester vase decorated with encrusted flowers on a marbled light-green ground, gilt handles and square base, 9¾ inches, and a Chamberlain's vase, 8¾ inches, painted with flowers, richly gilt scrolled borders £42

3 Worcester dishes of the Wall period, with shaped borders printed in under-glaze blue with medlars and flowers, 8½ inches, 9 similar plates, 3 saucer-dishes, and 4 other dishes £19

2 oval pierced Worcester baskets printed with medlars and flowers, 1 circular basket, 7¾ inches, 3 junket dishes moulded in relief and decorated in similar style £20

'King of Prussia' Worcester baluster mug signed 'R. H. Worcester' and an anchor, 6 inches, and another smaller, similarly signed £10

Caughley cabbage-leaf mask-lipped jug decorated with flowers in underglaze blue, 8½ inches, 2 others 7½ inches and 9½ inches, and a small mug £9

Such were the ruling prices when I began to think about refilling my empty cabinets. The question was, what with? I decided I had to have colour, for mahogany goes well with polychromes. I toyed for a time with the idea of collecting figures, not the early, terribly expensive ones of Bow or Chelsea (though I had indeed bought a fine Bow figure of 'Winter' for £20), but the later, equally well-modelled ones of the Chelsea–Derby period. Then something happened to put me off. A certain dealer whom I knew very well traded for the most part in second-hand furniture, but very occasionally he did find some nice bits of china. Moreover, he never bought them unless they were cheap. A few days after a big Cotswold sale a mutual friend came up to me in the street.

'I hear your pal Smith [as I will call him] had a good day at the Cambrai sale! D'ye know what he bought?'

Well, I did not know, but I lost no time in going along to his shop to find out.

No sooner had I entered than another fellow stepped in, who I knew to be a Polish buyer for the States export trade. There was a lot of fresh stuff about, I could see, and I edged into the back room. There, among a table-full of Berlin and Dresden figures and noisy, fussy candelabras, I spotted three fine pieces of Chelsea-Derby, a cupid with a basket of flowers, complete with a fine bocage, a tall figure of 'Europe' from the set of the Continents, and a graceful figure of a girl. I decided to go to £5, £10, and £4 respectively, and to lie low until the buyer had gone.

To my horror he, too, edged into the back room!

I hung on.

Smith signalled to me to wait—but it was only to explain that he had bought the whole lot for £45, acting on the buyer's instructions. He couldn't offer me a single piece! All or nothing was the arrangement, and they had all been bought as continental!

My next thought was, how about pottery figures? Now, of course, when Astbury and Whieldon made their figures they were intended to be sold as mantelpiece ornaments for a few coppers each, and I knew that they could sometimes be picked up at very low prices. I remembered Pease and his horseman! And I myself had already had one experience of that kind of thing in a Devonshire village.

I was on holiday at the time, before the war, and I called in a lonely farmhouse, miles from anywhere, for a drink of milk. The farmer, an uncouth, crafty-looking lout of a fellow, asked me civilly enough to sit for a few minutes in the kitchen. I was glad to do so, because it was a drizzly, cold sort of day, and I was tired.

I had hardly sat down when on the high mantelpiece I spotted a fairish Toby jug, not an early one, but well-modelled and decorated with splashes of blue and reddish-brown. I suppose it was Leeds.

'That's a pretty jug up there,' I said casually.

'Ah!' said the farmer, 'belonged to my father, that did. There's some more in the front room, but I don't set much store on it. The missus likes it though.'

I tried hard to hide my excitement. This was the kind of thing I had dreamed about!

'Can I have a look at it?' I asked.

'No harm in that,' was the reply, and I was led into the front room, where he opened the door of a large oak corner-cupboard.

I nearly dropped! In the centre of the middle shelf stood a Whieldon Toby, complete with his hat, and glowing softly with smudgy mazarine and green. On one side of him there was a magnificent pigeon, probably by Ralph Wood, and on the other an agate-ware cat in white and slaty-blue, with a grey mouse in his mouth. The other two shelves were filled with pipers, sweeps, and other early models, all in colour, and all either Whieldon or Ralph Wood. It was a wonderful sight.

I handled a piece or two as carelessly as I could.

Then, equally carelessly, 'Ever think of selling them?' I asked.

He pushed his cap to one side and scratched his sandy head.

'Well now, I don't know as 'ow I 'ad. We likes to see 'em there, like, though they'm ugly enough old things. What should you say they'm worth?'

That was a poser! It was not so much what they were worth, as much as what I could afford to give for them! I thought quickly. I supposed I might run to £50 or so.

'Oh, about fifty pounds, I should think,' I said.

The farmer looked at me and his jaw dropped. He gulped. Then:

'You mean you'll give me fifty pounds for them images in that cupboard?'

'And the jug on the mantelpiece thrown in. Yes,' I replied.

'Well, I'll be damned!' he exclaimed. He walked across to the open door and shouted up the staircase.

'Missus! Missus! Come down a minute!' Then, turning to me, 'She'll be down in a minute, and we'll see what she has to say.'

Sure enough there were footsteps on the stairs, and in came his wife, wiping her hands on her apron. Her husband told her what it was all about, and she looked at me curiously. They stepped outside and I could hear them whispering. This went on for a few minutes, and I heard her going back upstairs again. Then in came the farmer.

He hesitated, coughed once or twice. Then he said, 'My missus says if they'm worth all that money they might be worth a lot more. They've been there for a long time now, and it won't do no harm for 'em to stop there a bit longer!'

We argued for half an hour but it was no use. All the way home I wanted to kick myself for being so honest. Or, at least, as honest as I could afford to be. I'd probably have had the lot for £5.

It is not always an easy matter to put a price on rarities. One day when I called in to see Owen Wheeler I found a dealer already there. He had brought two sets of ivory chessmen and I sat and listened. To beguile my time Wheeler threw over a few small bundles of fifteenth- and sixteenth-century spoons, bronze and lateen. I had never seen the like. When his visitor had gone, 'What are they worth?' I asked.

'Well, what are they worth?' he echoed. 'Who's to put a value on them? I wouldn't miss this lot for worlds—and yet their owner hasn't the foggiest idea what to charge for them!'

Wheeler was fond of putting a piece down before me, on which I had to gaze, and ponder, and learn. Sometimes I took a new piece to show him. If he thought anything of it he would say so, but if not he would glance at it, put it down on the table and talk about something else. Before I left I would put it surreptitiously in my pocket.

Of course that was only if it was something I had bought for myself. At one time he told me he was looking for marked Nantgarw porcelain for a friend, and a few weeks later, as duty bade me, I asked him to pay £7 5s. od. for a marked 'NANTGARW C.W.' plate with plain moulded edges and a central 'Coalport' bouquet of rather scratchy execution. He merely swore. 'Five quid would be ample.' Dear at that, I thought, but as it was on approval all was well.

Whenever I see chessmen I think of Wheeler, because until he died I played that wonderful game with him once or twice every month, on Saturdays. He was living in rooms in Worcester, and his sitting-room was filled with his own lovely bits of furniture. I can picture it now. On the mantelpiece were two large covered vases of lignum vitae and two goblets to match, their graceful outlines repeated in the alternate light yellow and dark brown of the grain. A small Chippendale bachelor's chest housed his collection of early British stamps (and I knew that in the bottom drawer were some lovely small pieces of K'hang H'si blue and white), and upon it stood a great bowl of polished elm, hard as steel. Opposite the fireplace stood a very large Elizabethan oak chest, inlaid with holly, bog-oak, and mother-of-pearl, and on either side of a miniature Chippendale drop-leaf table with slender turned legs stood two of a set of perfect Queen Anne fiddle-back walnut chairs. The rest were still stored in the shop of the dealer from whom he had bought them. I remember that he had astonished the locals by paying, I think, £500 for the set of twelve. They said he'd never see his money again, and of course he never did, though not in the sense they had intended.

As soon as I arrived out would come the chess-board, and he would hold out two pawns, a white and a black, in two shaking, mittened hands. I would choose, and we would set to, one on either side of the big table.

We used to play all the morning, the atmosphere so thick with tobacco smoke that you could have cut it with a knife, until the lunch was brought in. It was always mutton chops. No sooner had we eaten than on we went again, until tea-time was the signal for me to leave. I won only very occasionally, for he was a devil with his pawns!

I have digressed enough, for one thing leads to another. I do not quite know why I decided finally to collect Chamberlain's, Flight's and Grainger's Worcester. I had always deplored its ostentation. And yet, when I began to think, the skill of the artists was some compensation for that fault. It was only that I had to get used to concentrating upon decoration instead of upon pastes and glazes. There is a certain kind of fascination, too, in the kind of marks, that are almost documents, that were used at the later Worcester factories. And I knew that unmarked pieces could still be bought fairly cheaply, apart from the fact that my wife agreed that the first few bits I bought looked very well in the cabinets.

Cabinet arrangement is a most important thing. I always had Con's dreadful example as an object-lesson in how not to do it. Not that his pieces were always in such a turmoil as I had first seen them, because every time Wheeler visited him nothing would do but that he must 'blow them up,' as he put it, and for a few weeks there was some sort of order on the shelves. It never lasted long.

I found no great difficulty in finding good pieces, for apart from my week-end trips it was not long before dealers were sending pieces on approval. The news spreads quickly. Pease in particular was most attentive, and I only sent one piece back to him. It is well known that Wall period figures are extremely rare, and the same applies almost as much to the Chamberlain years. I had found a nice little reclining ram, in white on a base covered with matt cobalt-blue enamel, and before I was interested in them I handled two specimens of 'Just Breeched,' the figure of a boy in long trousers, one in white biscuit and the other enamelled, but no sooner had I begun to collect in real earnest than figures disappeared, apparently, from the market! So when a postcard came from Nottingham with information of a purchase of a lady in crinolines, I replied by return and asked for it to be sent. Along it came, beautifully packed as usual, and at first I was quite delighted. Unfortunately, closer examination revealed that the whole of the crinoline had been cleverly 'made up'. I hoped he had not paid too much for it, for unusual pieces do command high prices. The first important piece of Chamberlain's porcelain I bought was a case in point.

One Sunday afternoon I was in Broadway, the very last place one would expect to find a bargain. A Derby dealer I knew (from whom I had bought my big cabinet) had just opened up, and my purpose was to find him. This was not easy, because it seemed that there had been considerable opposition to yet another new dealer in the place, and at that time he had not been able to put up his sign. I found the house at last, a lovely old place lying well back from the road in a typical Cotswold walled garden. With no thought of buying I looked round his showrooms, seeing nothing to tempt me, but as I was leaving I happened to ask whether he had any Flight's or Chamberlain's Worcester. I thought I was safe because I had seen none! He led me to his private room, and there on a table was a magnificent basket standing on four scrolled legs, pierced, with ornate gilt handles. Inside the bottom was a well-painted bouquet of flowers, the sides were painted with gold sprays on a pale salmon-pink ground, and the flat rim was covered with applied sea-shells, brightly enamelled and intricately moulded. My friend said he had bought it privately only that day, and had just finished washing it. No one else had seen it, and the price (to me, and I have little doubt to anyone else!) was £65.

I had walked away a hundred yards or so along the street before I began to regret not having bought it. I retraced my steps, reached the garden gate, and again walked away. This I did several times. The last time I went inside and made out a cheque. I almost wished someone else had seen it first. And yet, when the collection was sold a few years later, it fetched £95. For of course I did sell, for the second time and for the same reason. Just as to everyone comes a time when he must draw on his savings, so a collector, who hasn't any as a rule, has to realize on what he has. But before that time came, the new attraction led to many new contacts and new ventures.

Among the many well-known examples of Flight's Worcester in the museums are pieces of what is commonly known as the 'Nelson' service. The legend was that the model for the female figure on the sea-shore, in a different pose on every piece, was Lady Hamilton, and the service was made to Nelson's order. Now the works records are known to indicate quite clearly that it was in fact made in 1792 for the Duke of Clarence, and that the painting was done by James Pennington. How, then, did the legend begin? I found a reasonable explanation quite by chance, for I bought a plate for £20. On the back was pasted a large label that was evidently part of the page of a sale catalogue. Lot No. So-and-so, it said, was part of a service 'made to the order of Lord Nelson.' That is the way in which errors are born and perpetuated, for the written word is all too often accepted as fact.

Another piece was shown to me one day, a large bowl decorated with Nelson's coat-of-arms and with the dates of some of his victories written on ribbons. One of the dates was wrong! I decided the piece must be Chinese, and I began a long correspondence with various dealers, with Sothebys, and with the National Maritime Museum at Greenwich in order to sort out the truth of the matter. Mr. George Naish, of the Museum, wrote to say that he had several pieces of the same service, as well as many other pieces with Nelson associations, and would I care to go and see what he had. My wife and I accepted eagerly, and Mr. Naish showed us round. Among other treasures we stood spellbound before a great showcase filled with the splendid service of which I had a single plate. A blaze of burnished gold and mazarine blue, tureens, dishes, plates, sauce-boats, the whole lot. When it is remembered that many pieces are scattered about the country I cannot imagine the size of the original single service.

Cabinets were opened for us by an attendant, we handled piece after piece, and at last our guide took us to a store-room not open to the public. In the cupboards were parts of other services, some of them quite unknown to me, as well as hundreds of odd pieces, every one of which had some association with Nelson. Above all, in a glass case was the original inventory of the hero's Merton house, written in a beautiful, flowing longhand of the kind rarely seen nowadays. Before we left Mr. Naish promised to have several pages photographed for me, as well as those pieces of pottery and porcelain that I selected. He was as good as his word, and by their aid I was able shortly afterwards to pass on to other collectors much of what I had learned.

There is, of course, a wealth of Nelson relics of all kinds up and down the country, both in museums and in private hands. I met one such enthusiast through the medium of my book on 'blue and white.' Captain Derek Cooper, retired from Her Majesty's Navy, lived in Surrey, and he first wrote to me regarding some of the pieces I had illustrated, of which he had duplicates. Several letters passed, and eventually I was invited to go down to spend a week-end in order to see his collection.

I found a lovely, long, low house set amid spacious age-old lawns, shadowed by enormous cedars. A quiet, peaceful spot, though not far removed from the busy London–Southampton road. Inside, as I quickly found, were treasures of every kind, furniture, pictures, engravings, and above all, fine china. I was told that all these, and indeed much more, had been inherited from a well-known collector, a member of the Ceramic Circle, and that my host had not been in time to prevent the burning of a lot of rubbish that had included a pile of old sale catalogues and the back numbers of that Circle's valuable 'Transactions'!

The blue and white was lovely. Not only was there so much of it, but also it was so beautifully arranged as part of the house, and every piece, almost, was a rarity. In the dining-room I admired two great bow-fronted William and Mary walnut cabinets chock-full of powder-blue Bow. Some of the pieces were decorated with Chinese garden scenes, and upon the big vase which stood upon a table to fill the centre of each scene the word BOW was clearly drawn. This was rarity indeed! I saw a stately pair of Chelsea vases, the epitome of that great factory's final attainment, a magnificent chest in coloured lacquer that had been rescued from a cottager who filled his oil-lamps upon its lid, and a Nelson collection that included not only a host of mugs and jugs, but also enamelled patch-boxes, a large bust in Nottingham stoneware, and an even larger one cast in lead that I think must be quite unique and probably a true likeness second to none. I ate my dessert from green-bordered plates made at Worcester in the 1760s, and I was lulled to sleep that night by the gentle ticking of a little bracket-clock by Quare that stood upon my bedroom mantelpiece. What more could a collector desire?

My hobby has led me into pleasant places, but when I think back I have no happier memories than of sitting after dinner with my kind host and hostess, on a warm summer's evening, in the shade of the great cedars. I see in memory the first bats flitting overhead as the shadows lengthen across the lawn, and I feel a part of a gracious age that is gone. Sometimes I creep in my dreams down the great staircase, across the empty library to where the morning sun makes patches of silver on the dewy grass. I find a rustic seat and there I sit alone until at length from the front door emerges a great tabby cat. He pauses awhile to stretch and yawn. He washes himself in difficult places. Then at last he pretends to see me for the first time, and crosses to where I sit, very deliberately with his tail in the air, to lie at my feet. 'Good morning, Comus,' I say to him, and he blinks at me and lies on his back to show that we are friends.

It is sad to know that all museums are not so well kept as that of Greenwich. Some years ago I visited a provincial one to look at the work of a particular porcelain painter. I knew that there ought to be a great deal to admire, because the place had once been famous for its pottery. So there was, but I was not prepared for what I found. The galleries were well kept, though to be sure the emphasis was on pictures, but I have never seen anything like the store-rooms. Every wall was lined with glass-fronted cupboards, every one chock-full of filthy porcelain. The floor was crowded with show-cases and trestle tables, and each looked for all the world as though its once lovely contents had been poured out of a bucket. What was worse, as I walked across the room broken china crunched beneath my feet.

I know, of course, that museum authorities are hampered by lack of space and by the impossibility of employing an adequate staff. It is impossible to show all their possessions at the same time, and some must needs be stored. Nevertheless, that experience did much to persuade me that no collection of mine would ever be left to a museum! You and I, and the museums, too, are but custodians, for a short space of time, of something we keep in trust for those that come after, and it is our duty to keep faith.

At the other extreme there are those museums who are able to display all that they have. When I was quite a lad I remember visiting the Works Museum of the Royal Worcester Porcelain Company. A brief glance at its contents was part of the tour of the works, and our guide was a very old man, an old employee. Here and there, we noticed, were signs whose bold lettering forbade the giving of any kind of gratuity to the guides. Our old fellow stopped with his back to one of them, and with a backward flick of his thumb 'You don't want to take no notice of them!' he said.

I visited the museum many times afterwards, especially while I was collecting Worcester porcelain. The fact that it was rebuilt and rearranged some years ago has made it doubly attractive. The collection is particularly rich in the early nineteenth-century wares, and I was intrigued by the amazing variety of the Grainger ones. Like Spode, that factory attempted everything. The new curator, Mr. Cyril Shingler, did all he could to help me in my studies. Aided and abetted by the directors he opened the cabinets and allowed me to take photographs. He even unearthed for me the old Grainger and Chamberlain pattern-books, and they were a treat indeed! If only greater care had been taken at all our potteries of such priceless things! Spodes have theirs, and so has the present Coalport management, but they are the exceptions. And yet surely the most ignorant could see that by reason of their lovely, meticulous work in water-colour, and the wealth of information they afford, they were well worth keeping?

I went to see Mr. Dyson Perrins to find out whether he had anything in that line to show me, and he told me that shortly after he took control he came upon a party of workmen burning a pile of ledgers in a back-yard. He rescued all he could, and I was allowed to see them. Or at least he left me to my own devices in a room whose walls were lined with shelves, each of which was piled high with dusty volumes. Among the interesting things I found, perched high on a rickety pair of steps, were Stock Books from 1788 to 1795, Invoice Books from Chamberlain to Turner of Caughley and from Turner to Chamberlain, from 1788 to 1843, Journals, Order Books, Cash Books relating to the sales both at Bond Street and at Worcester, Wages Books, and Letter Books. Some day someone will find time to explore them, and well worth while it will be, for this is the kind of thing I found, an extract from the Bond Street Journal referring to the sale of porcelain to Flight, Barr and Barr, for the various branches evidently kept their finances separately.

31st May 1821.
    Messrs. Flight, Barr & Barr, Worcester.
    3 Plates to pattern with Crest

    Messrs. Barr, Flight & Barr.

	£	s.	d.
4 large Fluted Bk. Cups & Saucers	1	15	0
2 Coffees		6	0
1 Roll Tray		18	0
1 Bread Dish		9	0
1 Six Cup Egg Stand	1	16	0
1 Tripod Comport		12	6
	5	16	6

    124 Yellow Band, Gold Line, Sprigs.

I was interested to find that even such a powerful firm as Chamberlain's did not scorn to sell their wares piecemeal at the local inns, or to hire them out for parties! Here are two extracts, from a Journal, that refer to such practices.

April 25th 1795.
    Thos. Weaver—Hoppole, Worcester, for Mrs. Danby, Swinton Park, near Ripon, Yorkshire.

	£	s.	d.			
12 Cups and Saus. Dejeuney handles broad gold edges. No. 63	3	3	0			
12 Breakfast plates do. at 2/6	1	10	0			
Package		2		4	15	0

May 31st 1821.
    Prince of Sax-Coburg

	£	s.	d.			
Hire of 6 Doz. Desert Plates and 6 Doz. Cups and Saucers for three different parties at 20/– each	3	0	0			
2 Cups broken, Brown Landscape		14	0			
1 Plate Grey and flowers broken		8		4	2	0

Antiques are so much more interesting when one can read about the everyday anxieties and problems of those who made them. But one worry, at least, was spared the early nineteenth-century employer of labour. He ruled his workers with a rod of iron! If they transgressed they were fined, and it was very easy to transgress, as the following copy of the Chamberlain rules and regulations for the year 1851 will show.

RULES AND REGULATIONS TO BE OBSERVED BY ALL PERSONS EMPLOYED IN THIS MANUFACTORY

TIME	CONDUCT
1 All Persons employed in this Factory to assemble at HALF-PAST SIX O'CLOCK throughout the year.	1 SWEARING and BAD LANGUAGE strictly forbidden at all times.
2 BREAKFAST-TIME, HALF-PAST EIGHT to NINE.	2 During work hours SILENCE and ORDER are required, and at all times steadiness and propriety of conduct recommended.
3 DINNER HOUR, ONE to TWO P.M.	3 SOBRIETY, CIVILITY, and PUNCTUALITY are indispensable for length of service.
4 Every day's work reckoned to terminate at SIX P.M.	4 Useful reading at proper times approved. All Immoral Publications and Prints found in the Works DESTROYED and their Owners DISCHARGED.

TIME	CONDUCT
5 All work not ready to be passed through the Warehouse by SIX O'CLOCK, P.M. on Friday, not reckoned for until the week following.	**5** 'ON NO PRETENCE WHATEVER' is intoxicating drink, of any description, allowed in the Works, and smoking is strictly prohibited.
6 Half an Hour allowed for assembling in a Morning, after which the Entrance Door will be locked, and a Quarter of an Hour at Breakfast and Dinner (except to day men).	**6** Such of the hands as take meals on the premises, are required to do so in their respective workshops, or in the case of Girls in the room appropriated to their exclusive use.
7 On Saturdays, Manufacturing labour to cease at FOUR P.M., from which time to hour for paying Wages, hands to employ themselves in cleaning rooms and benches, putting tools &c., in order throughout the Works.	**7** Any person found loitering in another Working Room will be fined unless he can give satisfactory reasons.
8 Wages commence paying at FIVE O'CLOCK, P.M., on Saturdays throughout the year.	**8** Boys are not allowed to play on the Premises.

March 1st, 1851.

I wonder what was meant by 'Immoral Publications or Prints'? There were no 'pin-up girls' in those days, no distracting calendars, and no paper-covered novels. And what was 'useful reading'?

Soon after I had begun to make my second collection the idea came to me of writing a book about the decoration of porcelain. After all, I thought, whereas the collector is bound to be interested in such things as factory history, pastes and glazes, and techniques, it is decoration that appeals to the ordinary man or woman who loves to have beautiful things without knowing very much about them.

When it was time to collect suitable photographs together the hard work really began. I think it is a mistake to illustrate a book about antiques with museum specimens. Apart from the fact that they have been reproduced so many times they are for the most part of a kind that is quite out of reach to the average collector, who wants to see pictures of which he can say, 'Ah, yes! I've got one just like that!'

I wrote to many famous dealers in London and in the provinces, and almost without exception they sent photographs that were first class because they had been properly taken by professionals. I did have a little trouble with one Wigmore Street man. When I wrote to him first I was out of engraved letter-heading, and I had no reply to a letter written on blank paper, with a typed address. I tried again, this time in better style. He replied most indignantly. How could I expect to be treated with respect if I did not write properly? 'No proper notepaper, no standing, nothing,' said he. But then he continued to say that of course he would be glad to help me, now that he knew I had proper notepaper! And so he did, and when the book appeared five of his best pieces were illustrated in it.

My own rapidly growing collection furnished most of the illustrations of later Worcester, and many collector friends rallied round. But still I had not enough material from which to choose, and in a happy moment of inspiration I wrote to Spodes at Stoke-on-Trent. Mr. Gresham Copeland replied, inviting me to visit the works, and on the appointed day I walked through the old iron gates into the eighteenth century.

I cannot believe that Mr. Copeland's office had changed since the days when Josiah Spode sat, surely, at the same table, in the same dusty little room, at the top of the same flight of narrow, wooden stairs. He must have crossed the floor so many times to look down through the little window-panes at the cobbled yard beneath, or to look up with pride at the selfsame towering kilns, terrifying almost in their sheer, conical smoothness. As we toured the work-rooms together I could see that little had been changed. It seemed sacrilege to have built an electric oven in such a place. And wherever we went I noticed an air of contented craftsmanship, and every man, it seemed, was known to his director by his Christian name. Is it a foolish fancy, I wonder, to suppose that the old order in industry is only to be found in places where lovely things are still made in the same traditional ways?

There are two museums at the Spode works, one belonging to the works and the other that of Mr. William Copeland himself. I was made free of both of them. 'Just make a note of the pieces you would like to have photographed, and I'll see to it,' said my host, and with that he left me to my browsing. The works collection, in particular, included every kind of ware ever made by the company, right from the beginning, and I soon found that almost any unmarked piece of early nineteenth-century bone-china could without much fear of contradiction be identified as Spode. Few patterns had not been attempted at one time or another. I had found the same thing when I first saw Mr. Dyson Perrins's Worcester collection, but, of course, whereas his pieces were identifiable by reason of differences of paste and glaze as Worcester and as nothing else, here at Stoke-on-Trent, the home, almost, of standardization, there was no clue but that afforded by pattern or, or course, by marks.

When I had seen everything there was to see I presented a formidable list of pieces. It was so difficult to narrow down my choice. The outcome was that within a few weeks a batch of fine photographs arrived, each accompanied by a typed description. Not only that, for a brand-new process had been used to produce two brilliant transparencies in full colour that were to be used for my dust-cover and frontispiece.

About that time I was in the throes of leaving the teaching profession, after twenty-five years of schoolmastering, in favour of industry. Some months before I had been introduced to a well-known industrialist who was also a collector of early Staffordshire pottery. This ever-young yet elderly man had the happy knack of being able to forget his business worries, and at the close of day to devote all his tenacity, shrewdness, and unerring sense of what is worth while to the building up of what must be one of the finest collections of perfect pieces in the country. At first I was content to handle and admire the Astbury, Whieldon, and Ralph Wood treasures that glowed behind the doors of an enormous Hepplewhite cabinet, but soon afterwards I was asked if I would photograph some of the finest pieces with a view to a written account of the collection in a collectors' magazine. I did so, and it was duly published. After that it was natural that, having decided to change my profession, I should ask my new friend for help and advice. Both were quickly forthcoming, and almost before I realized it blackboards, registers, and long holidays were a thing of the past.

Then one day when I had examined and admired a new acquisition, my friend said: 'Have you ever heard of a dealer by the name of Parsons?' (That is not his name, but it will serve.)

'Of course,' said I. 'He was as well known as Partridge twenty years ago, but I've no idea what has happened to him.'

'He had a shop in H—— a few years ago, but I understand he's left. But only last week I heard he had a place on the South Coast somewhere. See what you can find out, because I think he's got some good stuff!'

By a strange coincidence, only a week or so after I had a letter from a friend in Derby who had just returned from holiday at a little seaside fishing village. He told me all about his finds, and mentioned in passing that he had found a new dealer named Parsons, to whom he had been introduced by a young fellow and his wife, who had opened up near their lodgings. This was too good to be true! I wrote to them without delay, and by return came a letter saying that the Parsons in question was a relation of the man I was trying to trace, who did indeed live not so far away. He was retired, but still bought and sold from his private house, the address of which they gave to me. The hunt was up with a vengeance. I wrote another letter, and received by return a warm invitation to travel down to see him. He finished up by saying, 'Bring your bathing costume with you in case we get some sun!'

I reached the little seaside village in time for tea, and soon found the house I was seeking, a little white house perched high upon a jutting rock right in the very middle of a wide bay. The door was opened by a rather thin, stooping man of a little above medium height, severe-looking and spectacled, who turned out to be Parsons himself. I told him who I was. 'Are you a dealer, or what?' he asked. I told him about myself, and from then on all was plain sailing. I soon accustomed myself to his plain speaking—he said exactly what he thought and damn the consequences—and we got on together like a house afire.

My friend at home was quite right about the Staffordshire pottery; I had never seen so many unusual pieces in any one place, but that was not all. Porcelain of every kind, salt-glaze in brilliant colours, delft, it was all there, most of it in the cabinets that lined one wall of a long, cool room whose windows faced the sea. Above all (for first impressions last long) I saw the largest Chelsea 'Fable subject' round dish I had ever seen, and a magnificent, stately pair of Meissen vases of the Augustus Rex period, painted with Chinese subjects by Löwenfinck and J. H. Herold in reserves on a yellow ground. Most wonderful of all he showed me, in a little glass case all to itself, the porcelain head of a little child, the very personification of vivacious youth. This was Chelsea, a model of the head of his daughter by the great sculptor Roubiliac himself. Some pieces there are that are so rare and perfect that no price can be set upon them: £1,000 or £15,000, who is to say? But apart from monetary value I doubt whether a more perfect piece of porcelain exists today, and it was found in a junk-shop.

After supper that first evening I was shown a collection, almost complete, of Air Mail stamps. I have never been able to rouse up much enthusiasm over postage-stamps—their beauty must perforce for the most part remain unseen—but these were exceptional as regards colour and perfected printing. The Russian and Egyptian ones were especially remarkable. The whole collection was arranged in very unusual albums, I think of French origin and practically unobtainable, in which a separate space was reserved for each stamp. I noticed that very few were empty.

After I had been shown everything we sat down together before the fire, and Parsons told me of his eventful, adventurous life, of buying trips in every part of the Continent, of great collectors of the past. He took me behind the scenes. He told me, too, that although his doctors had ordered him to retire he could not bear to do so, and every now and then he would leave his quiet retreat to visit again the London sale-rooms, or to fly off at a moment's notice to Paris, Berlin, Rome, or some other of the great continental cities.

It was very late when finally I was taken up to my little bedroom. I slept soundly, and awoke next morning to the soft murmur of the sea on the rocks 50 feet below my window. I leapt out of bed, and leaned out to look over the blue sea, as calm as a millpond, to the distant headlands at either end of the bay. The thought crossed my mind that the little rock on which the house was built was for all the world like the nose in the middle of a fancy Worcester crescent mark.

After my first visit I always took my camera with me, but there were so many pieces to photograph that I always had to change the plates in my slides. Now since there was no dark-room that had to be done in my bedroom, with the curtains drawn. Even then, except on the darkest night, stray rays of light would get in, and I found out how to work in a wardrobe with the doors almost closed. The first time I did this my host half-opened the bedroom door to make some inquiry about my comfort. Of course the landing light was on and I yelled 'DON'T COME IN, WHATEVER YOU DO!' so violently that he hastily shut the door and retreated in disorder. What he thought I was up to I don't know, but I explained the next morning, and all was well.

Sometimes we went out together in my car. We called on the young couple with the new antique shop, whom he was helping with advice. When they bought unwisely he did not choose his words! I remember they had some very fine strawberries in the little garden at the back of the house, and I was introduced to a wonderful long drink made of cider and brandy, laced with slices of that most delicious of all English fruits.

I have mixed memories of one long trip that was made in order to collect a Victorian doll from the antique shop where it had been left awaiting collection. It was the biggest doll I have ever seen, at least 3 feet long, but to cap it all it was fixed in a coffin-shaped glass case of considerable weight and fragility. We sweated for half an hour (and it was a hot summer's day) to get it through the car door and on to the back seat. This done, we re-entered the shop for a look round. Everything was unspeakably filthy, it was the worst kind of junk-shop, but we both knew that it was also just the sort of place where something good might be picked up. Sure enough, under a pile of old saddles and harness in a dark corner, we saw the gleam of what looked like white china of some kind. I lifted up the rubbish and Parsons lugged out what turned out to be a pair of large heraldic shields, moulded in low relief, and apparently made of some kind of stoneware. They were so dirty that it was difficult to be sure. I thought them ugly and worthless, but Parsons apparently thought otherwise, for he bought them for £2, and I could see that he was excited. No sooner had we got into the car than 'I bet you don't know what they are!' he exclaimed. I agreed. I was interested only in getting home to have a bath. 'Dwight's stoneware!' he shouted. 'I knew he made 'em but I've never seen one before. Worth a mint of money!'

He jabbered about his filthy plaques all the way home, and no sooner were we indoors than he had to take them under the kitchen tap and set to work with a scrubbing-brush. At first, as he worked, he declaimed loudly about the merits of John Dwight's stoneware, of its wonderful whiteness, the remarkable modelling, and so on. But gradually, as the water in the sink grew blacker and blacker, he said less and less, and began to grunt to himself. Then he looked at me sideways. 'Have you got a pen-knife?' he said. I passed it over. He seemed suddenly to make up his mind, and grimly he hacked away at one corner of the now white and glistening 'stoneware.' Lo and behold, a piece came away as though it had been cheese. It was plaster of Paris!

Without a single word he picked up the two frauds and marched with them into the garden. I followed him, trying to look serious, as befitted the occasion. At the bottom of the garden was a little brook, and it had a very deep, rocky bed. He held his plaques high over his head and hurled them down with all his force, then turned on his heel and marched back to the house, still without a word. Neither of us ever mentioned Dwight's stoneware from that day to this, but it was encouraging to me to realize that Homer sometimes nods.

Nine

As I write these words it is just five years since the time came to sell what had slowly become quite a representative collection of later Worcester porcelain. A few pieces were sold to friends, and the rest I took to Gloucester to be sold together with someone else's silver in the ballroom of a large hotel. I am often asked how best to sell antiques, and I am never sure what to advise. Single pieces, of course, can be offered to a dealer but only if the vendor has some idea of the price he is prepared to accept. In any case the right sort of dealer must be carefully chosen, because a specialist knows his customers and is in a position to offer a higher price than would be given by a general dealer. When the latter is considering a purchase he thinks not only 'How much is this worth?', or even 'How much can I get for it?'; more important to him, by far, is the answer to the question 'How long is it likely to remain in my shop?' In my own case I decided against a London saleroom, because nowadays more and more London dealers are attending likely provincial sales, and are more likely to buy than they would be on their home ground. They do not care to return empty-handed, and very often their determination to outbid the locals causes them to push up the prices.

I wrote my own catalogue descriptions, and in this regard I would always advise the ordinary auctioneer that a fee paid to an expert is money well spent. Not very long ago a local auctioneer told me that he had been commissioned to dispose of the contents of a cottage, and asked me whether I would go with him to identify the china and glass, of which there was a great deal. I did so willingly, to find many pieces that I knew would fetch high prices if only the right people could be attracted to the sale. I advised that he should allow me to write the descriptions, and that copies of the catalogue should be widely circulated. He agreed, and when I had done I asked what sort of a figure, in his experience, might be realized. He glanced through my list and suggested, as I remember, about £900. A month later, on the day of the sale, the village swarmed with London and provincial dealers. The pubs did a wonderful trade, and a farmer opened a field as a car-park at half a crown a car. The upshot was that the Londoners banded together against the locals to such purpose that the sum realized was more than three times the estimated figure. Prices were not silly, but they were more than satisfactory to auctioneer and vendor alike.

As for my own collection, many pieces did indeed go straight to London, but here again, because a score or so failed to reach my reserves, I learned another important fact. They were included, a few weeks later, in a large country-house sale of effects which included a lot more china of all kinds. To my surprise I was able to stand by and hear my same reserves handsomely exceeded. Why? Simply because they were judged by the company they kept! Even dealers, it seems, are apt to think that all that comes from a house of quality must necessarily be first class. At this same sale there was another example of the importance of correct cataloguing. Among the lots that were spread out on trestle tables in the large marquee was a pair of small, covered tureens painted with flowers, and described as Dresden. As I was looking at them a collector friend came up to me, and asked what I thought of them. 'Longton Hall,' said I, 'what do you think?' 'The same as you,' he said, 'and I'd like to buy them.' Well, since he was a wealthy man I left them to him, but I wished I hadn't when he secured them for £12, still as 'Dresden.' And that was in a tent with every dealer in the neighbourhood letting him get away with it!

It is all too easy to acquire the reputation of being an expert, particularly if one ventures into print. On the other hand, one can write simply for the love of it, without any desire for notoriety or fame and, perhaps, without deep knowledge. I have heard of one writer who has an enormous library of books on collecting, which he uses to turn out page after page of most illuminating and apparently erudite articles. I doubt whether he or indeed anyone else could ever pretend to such an all-embracing knowledge of antiques that his range of subjects would seem to indicate, but I have no quarrel with that, because he gives a great deal of pleasure and spreads so much knowledge. After all, what is a 'hack writer'? True, he may not offer startling theories (and so certainly is seldom guilty of instigating false ones) or set the collecting world afire, but does he not introduce many to delights they would otherwise never have enjoyed, paving the way, as it were, to more advanced reading and research? It may, perhaps, be a duty for the experienced to set the beginner's feet on the right path.

What, then, is an 'expert'? Let me relate, first, a story that was told to me, years ago, by an old dealer who was acknowledged by the trade as being second to none in his knowledge of old porcelain. I will try to tell it, as nearly as I can, in his own words.

'It came to my ears that a dealer on the Continent had for sale a very fine set of old *famille verte* vases and beakers, five to the set, and that he had offered them to another dealer, who we will call Smith, only to have them condemned as fakes. Now, Smith was supposed to know all about Chinese porcelain, and I thought no more about it until one day I called in to look at some Meissen figures. I completed my business, and just as I was leaving the shop the dealer asked me whether I would be interested in a set of *famille verte* vases. I said I would, and he took me into his private room. There they were, on a table, the selfsame pieces I had heard about. He said nothing about Smith, but I knew that the low price he asked was the result of his opinion. I was sure they were right as soon as I saw them, and I bought them.

'No sooner was I at home again than I asked Hobson of the V. & A. to come and see them. He did so, and gasped with amazement! I told him Smith had seen them, and he said, "Why on earth did he not buy them?"

'Encouraged by this opinion I sent off a long cable to an American millionaire who I knew collected really fine Chinese porcelain. Back came his reply—he had instructed his agent to come and see them.

'A few days later in walked Smith. He'd heard I had some vases, could he see them? "No," I said, "I'm not showing them to the trade," whereupon he took from his pocket a cable from the same millionaire.

' "Well," I said, "if you are acting for him I must show them to you."

'He looked at them very carefully, and finally he turned to me and said, "Did you know I had already declared them to be fakes?"

' "Yes," I replied, "but you know as well as I that they are perfectly genuine!"

'He looked rather shamefaced, and said, "I know, but I cannot alter my declared opinion. Don't tell anyone I'm agent for ——!"

'So the millionaire did not get the vases, which now stand in a very famous English mansion. Remember, always back your opinion, have confidence in yourself, and never forget that experts differ in their opinions as much as doctors!'

Every collector realizes that the more pieces he sees, and the more he reads, the more will he know his limitations. Nevertheless, an expert gives an opinion that is based on years of experience and study, although he knows full well that someone else can always be found who will as likely as not contradict it. I suppose it is true to say that the best of all expert opinions is the final judgement of those who sit around the table at Sothebys or Christies. They are backing their opinions with hard cash, and a hard fight is seldom fought out over anything that is not genuine. That is why it is good, if one can afford it, to buy from a London specialist, or even to be among those who make the final bids. Of course, there must be exceptions, and it is not so long ago that several hundreds of pounds were given, after keen competition, for a Toby jug that was declared by more than one expert to be a modern fake. Who is to know, for sure?

As I have already related, the first time I was called in as an expert was when I went to Chastleton, and since then I have photographed and described many other fine collections. The urge to write about something one loves is very strong. Besides, writing is one of the best ways of learning, and what could be more worth while than to draw attention to a collection that is 'on show,' and so to persuade others to share one's pleasure? There is something of the missionary in every collector, if the truth be told; he is so happy in his pursuit that he cannot understand the apathy of anyone else.

One of the finest great houses I have visited is Aynhoe Park, near Banbury, a lovely stone-built mansion remodelled by Sir John Soane in 1800, that stands four-square and enduring at the side of the curving high-road. I had been told that the owner, Mr. Richard Cartwright, had a notable collection of porcelain, and when I wrote to ask whether I might be permitted to write an illustrated account of it for the *Apollo* magazine he gladly consented.

The day began rather unfortunately. I remember it was a Tuesday. I drew up at the front door complete with my camera and floodlights only to find that I was not expected. The family was in London. Well, I knew I had not mistaken the day, and this was confirmed when I spoke to Mr. Cartwright on the telephone. He was very apologetic, and instructed his butler to attend to my wants and to give me all the help I needed. Actually I needed none, for I always find that well-meaning help is usually a hindrance. I would much sooner be left to myself. Accordingly, after he had given me a glass of sherry, the butler left me alone, and I soon found the lightest room for my purpose, in which I set up my camera and background. This was the 'Murillo Room,' the old orangery. It was so called because of the great *Ascension of the Virgin* that hung on one end wall. Next, I wandered from room to room, from cabinet to cabinet, trying to fix in my visual memory the appearance of each. I find that with practice this can quite easily be done, so that aided by careful notes and photographs I can recall the position and appearance of every piece when I sit down to write.

Every old house is bound to have a considerable quantity of old china, usually Chinese or Meissen bought at a time when only the rich could afford it, and when English porcelain was looked upon as a rather poor substitute. At Aynhoe I particularly admired a wonderful service found by General William Cartwright on the field of Waterloo, each piece painted with a different view of Dresden. It was complete with its travelling cases of red leather, and the assumption is that it was left behind by Napoleon. But above all I was quite entranced by the contents of the 'Chinese Room,' part of which had been Soane's 'Cold Bathroom.' Of all Oriental wares none is more beautiful than the 'monochromes,' but they are so rare that it is seldom that they are seen to proper advantage, that is, *en masse*. A single piece is attractive, but the impact on the senses of row upon row of them is almost overpowering. I entered, then, a large rectangular room whose walls were lined with brilliantly lit, arched recesses, lined with grey, and each filled with fine pieces of a single colour. There was the mirror-black or black-gold of the K'hang H'si period, sombre yet magnificent, the iron glazes of black, brown, and olive-green, the purples and lavenders, the russet and green-mottled peach-bloom, the rare Imperial yellow, the greens, the *rouge-de-fer*, the crimsons and, of course, the splendid *flambés* and the delicate *blanc-de-chine*. I would have liked to have photographed every piece, for every one was a gem.

I had hoped that I might be able to pay a return visit to Aynhoe, for the monochromes deserved separate treatment. Mr. Cartwright was willing, and it remained only for a date to be fixed. Then, one evening, I read in the paper that he and his son had been killed in a motoring accident. I thought how sad it was that I had been made free of the collection of a man I had never seen. He could have taught me so much.

I had not been surprised to find that there was nothing finer at Aynhoe than my own 'tea-dust' bowl, but I was so excited and thrilled at the sight of so much beauty that I decided to treat it as the nucleus of a collection of similar wares. Even as I decided I knew the extent of my impertinence. Chinese porcelain of any kind is a lifetime's study, and few Europeans really understand it. I knew also that fine pieces are uncommon and expensive, though at the same time I fancied that perhaps because the average dealer knows so little about it I might find an occasional one at the right price.

My first acquisitions were found in Torquay, where my wife and I were spending an autumn holiday. We spotted two fine vases covered with 'ox-blood' glaze in the window of a small shop, the inside of which looked (and smelt) like a Chinese temple. A few weeks later, when I wrote to ask whether the proprietor had any more similar pieces, he wrote to say that he had a tall vase in turquoise-blue. Should he send it on approval? I invited him to do so, and when it arrived I had a puzzle on my hands, a foretaste of things to come! The glaze was quite wonderful, a shimmering, opalescent greenish blue, crackled all over, and blobby at the base. The inside was burnt almost black, and ridged to the touch as though it had been built up in coils. I knew the piece was either very old indeed, or very modern. It might well have been Japanese. But try as I would I could find no one who could tell me, and finally, since the price was £20, I sent it back.

I soon realized that trying to collect something that one knows so little about is to invite trouble, but I did not give up because I discovered Mrs. Esmé Godkin. One of the most recent developments in the antique trade is the springing up of many more dealers who do their business entirely by post. I believe a dealer in silver began it some years ago. At any rate, Mrs. Godkin was prepared to send her treasures, and I bought a number of good pieces from her. That was all very well, but I was not satisfied with buying on another's knowledge, and when a year had passed, and I had found only a half-dozen pieces elsewhere, I gave up, and she took all I had. All, that is, save for a single large, bottle-shaped turquoise vase that I kept because it was so decorative. It cost me £7, and I bought it from an interior decorator.

Is an interior decorator an antique dealer? I often wonder. She from whom I bought my big vase combined an unerring flair for beauty and 'rightness' with a remarkable knack of buying (and, what is unusual in the trade, selling) at very low prices. Because she was a very fine judge of quality and craftsmanship she seldom bought a fake, but she was naturally preoccupied with decorative values and period, and did not trouble herself very much with provenance. Dear 'Mother Pat'! Completely unpractical and unbusinesslike, she lived in a world of her own, but was unbelievably generous to those she liked. Mention only, for instance, the intention to furnish a passage with Bartolozzi prints, and as likely as not she would bring one under her arm (and be sure it would be a lovely one!) with the careless remark, 'I thought it might look well in that corner.' Always, that is, if she approved of the idea! It was often very difficult to decide whether such offerings were gifts or sales, and it was even more difficult to inquire. Fortunately, her son knew her little ways, and every so often he would say to her, 'Mother, just what have you sold to so-and-so?' and along came a bill.

In Dornford Yates's classis *The House that Berry Built* there is a wonderful description of the sort of interior decorator that is best left alone, but it is a modern fashion to employ a genuine one to furnish a large house. But, however satisfactory the result, it can never be the same as if the furnishings had grown up with it. Such was Chastleton, and another place I visited quite recently that I felt had the same indefinable atmosphere of graciousness is Madresfield Court, the seat of the Earl Beauchamp. Yet again my purpose was to see and write about the porcelain. In this instance an introduction to His Lordship and his Countess was effected through a mutual friend, and plans for my visit were made comfortably over the luncheon table. But again, when the time came to work, something went wrong.

Around the Court there is a wide moat, and the old drawbridge has given place to a stone causeway leading into a long porch rather like that of a church, at the end of which is the inner, glass-panelled front door. Only, when I arrived, I could find no trace either of bell or knocker. I thought I might be more fortunate at the porch entrance that was covered with thick creeper of some kind. I know it is thick because of the time I spent in groping amongst the spiders for a bell-pull which, of course, was not there, either. Back to the door, feeling rather like a small boy with his nose glued to a sweet-shop window. I knocked, hard. I could see in the distance the servants going about their business, but they did not see me. I tried the door, which opened at my touch, but of course I did not dare to enter. Finally, on one of my many trips along the side of the moat to find a back entrance which was apparently non-existent, I caught sight of the Countess sitting in the library window. Again, she did not see me, and there I stood on the causeway, glaring at the window and concentrating with all my might. At last, telepathy won. She saw me, and before long the butler let me in. I had been outside exactly half an hour.

Some pieces there are that are seldom seen to best advantage under modern conditions. I knew that very large animals and birds had been modelled at Meissen by Kirchner and Käendler, much too large to be easily or conveniently displayed, but here, in the great hall, I found pairs of swans 16 inches in height, parrots, eagles, and cockatoos, some white and some brilliantly enamelled, and all of them set up high on cornice or cabinet top so that their beauty of line and proportion could be properly appreciated.

The contents of the great London museums are described and illustrated in well-written guides, but many a provincial museum has collections that are almost unknown but that are yet worthy of description. Many have made a speciality of pottery and porcelain, though pictures must naturally take pride of place. At Cheltenham, in 1923, the Berkeley Smith collection of Chinese porcelain was placed on permanent loan, and around it the then curator, Herdman, patiently built up what is now a fine miscellaneous collection. I had the pleasure of describing it for a collecting magazine and later, in the 'Chinese Room' that from the beginning was set apart for the Chinese wares, I sat apprehensively with Mr. William Lane, of the V. & A., on a ceramic Brains Trust, and many and extraordinary were the questions fired at us! Swansea is another place that has benefited from the generosity of a collector, but in this case not only was a collection given, but also the building in which to house it. The hope was expressed that 'the Gallery may become a recognized centre for art lovers, and a source of pleasure, guidance, and inspiration.' When I visited the museum to see the Glyn Vivian collection for myself and to introduce it to a wider public I was impressed by two things. First, so far as earthenware is concerned, it was Spodes all over again, in the sense that few patterns were not known to the Cambrian potters, and secondly, that there are very few pieces in existence of which it can be said, 'This was painted by Billingsley himself.'

Mention of the versatility of the Swansea potters leads me to yet another aspect of the 'expert's' work. Can any connoisseur really identify any and every piece of ware to his own satisfaction?

The answer is a definite 'No!' When once stoneware, salt-glaze, and delft had been ousted by standardized pastes and glazes many hundreds of potteries throughout the land, and particularly in the Potteries, were making exactly the same kind of wares, using the same kind of patterns. In the absence of marks it is impossible to tell them one from another, and that is why one has so often to fall back on the threadbare words, 'Staffordshire. We can get no nearer than that!' Now, if that is the position even when a piece can be examined at leisure, how much more difficult when it is a matter of giving an opinion on the strength of a written description aided, perhaps, by an inferior snapshot or a rough sketch! For sometimes that has to be done. For some years I had the task of answering 'Collectors' Enquiries' in the pages of a magazine. Every week I would receive a batch of questions, some illustrated, and some not. It is admittedly difficult for anyone not a collector to know just what sort of information is essential, but what can one say, or what useful attribution can be given, to a correspondent who writes, 'I have a little cream-jug, 5 inches high, painted in blue with flowers and little squiggles. Can you please tell me where it was made, and when?' There is really only one answer. 'Tell me everything, first, about the paste and glaze. Opaque or transparent, and what colour is it against a strong electric light? What colour is the glaze, is it thick or thin, and is it crazed? The potting, is it clumsy or fine, is the piece heavy or light for its size? What is the section through the foot-rim? Is the decoration painted or printed? Is the gilding dull or bright, and is it tarnished? Is the colour over or under the glaze? When you have told me all this, and anything else you may observe, then, and then only, can I look through your eyes, and feel through your fingers, and so give you a reasoned and reasonable answer.' I have often wondered whether it might not be possible for some journal to organize a service whereby actual pieces might be sent to an expert. True, he would have to do a great deal of unpacking and repacking, but he would certainly have the opportunity of handling what might very often turn out to be unusual pieces.

One day I opened an inquiry concerning an earthenware plate, painted in underglaze blue with a Chinese subject, having an unusual moulded edge, and bearing an impressed 'workman's mark.' I read it through, stretched out my hand, and picked up from my table an exact duplicate! Had I not known it was made at Swansea, on the evidence of yet another piece like it in the Swansea museum, I should without doubt have called it Staffordshire.

Only on one occasion did I ever actually examine a piece that was the subject of an inquiry An old friend bought an enormous clock, fully 2 feet in height, made at Dresden (not Meissen) not so long ago. It was covered with moulded flowers, and supported, I think, by not less than a dozen small figures of cherubs It was quite horrible. I told him, regretfully, that it was modern, and that it was not modelled, as he thought, by Käendler, but I could see he did not believe me. A few weeks later, to my amazement and joy, I read his inquiry about the selfsame piece, and of course my answer was almost word for word what I had already said. Of course, he was not to know that I was responsible for it. When I saw him again: 'I wrote to *The* —— about my clock, and they say just the same as you did!' Well, I had the kudos either way, and so I did not tell him the truth!

Longer ago than I care to remember I called one day to see Tipping, to find his desk littered with photographs and foolscap. He was red in the face, and his scanty sandy hair was ruffled 'My God, Stan!' he exclaimed, 'I'm up to my neck! I've got to write up these best pieces of a dozen London dealers, and it's got to be in the post tonight!' I wished him joy, and left him to it. The sequel to this was in October 1951, when I had a letter from the editor of *Apollo*.

'I wonder if you would care to concoct an article about these photographs; what in fact is wanted is a review of ceramics in the dealers' galleries, saying the best that can be said about them.'

The mantle of Elijah with a vengeance! Fortunately every piece (and there were fourteen of them) was so good that it was easy to 'say the best,' while none belonged to other than a fairly well-known class of ware. Of course, there had to be no mistakes, and I suppose I made none, for I had no angry letters.

I find it great fun to visit private houses in order to 'vet' collections. One lady I know has her own fine family pieces, but wherever she goes she scours the little shops and market stalls for cheap 'bargains.' These she puts aside until she has a table-full, when she telephones me to go over to tell her what is worth keeping. The rest she gives to American friends as Christmas presents, each with its little label, except for saucers which she uses as ashtrays, and colourful jugs or bowls set on one side for flowers. I always have to tell her what she should have given for each piece, and nothing pleases her more than to be able to tell me that she gave much less! Before I knew her she had bought a large, covered tureen, in the shape of a very green cabbage, for 30s. I do not know who was the more agitated, I when I saw it and heard its cost, or she when I told her it was early Chelsea, and worth three figures in pounds! She likes, too, to make her own guess at attribution and date before I make my own, and although she never takes the trouble to study it is surprising, lately, how often she is right Sometimes I am on dangerous ground, as when I said a little coffee-can was Flight's Worcester. 'Oh!' she said, 'but I've got another just like it, and you said that was Spode!' So she had, and so I did. But then, they both could have been either, as I explained.

Attributions are all very well, but when one is asked to give valuations it is quite another matter It simply cannot be done, such is fluctuation of demand and sale-room conditions. I was once asked to advise in connection with a part dessert service of marked Bristol porcelain that had been offered by a dealer to a rich lady. She read a list of the pieces, but did not tell me what was asked. What would be a fair price, she asked. I reckoned up the piece, so much for a plate, so much for a comport, and so on, plus a little extra because it was nearly a service, and the total seemed rather a lot. I told her what I thought, and she handed over the dealer's letter. I was right to within £10, but that was more by luck than by judgement!

One of the pleasantest ways of talking about one's collecting hobby is to lecture. The audience is bound to listen or, at least, to endure. When I first began to give talks about ceramics I used to take a selection of pieces with me, and to begin, 'Pass this piece round, but please do not drop it because it is worth so-and-so!' It wasn't, of course, but my trick always created the desired atmosphere of awe and respect. But apart from the risk and the labour of packing and unpacking an audience can see very little of a piece held aloft on a platform, and if specimens are displayed on a table, to be examined after the lecture, one needs eyes in the back of one's head if something is not to be damaged. So, although it is not often that I lecture nowadays, when I do I always insist that my listeners bring their own pieces which I try to identify and to talk about. In that way we get variety and I myself learn a great deal. For instance, it has long been accepted that Madeley porcelain never bears a factory mark. And yet, six months ago, among a miscellaneous collection on a trestle table in a Coalport hall, I identified a lovely little recumbent lion, gilded all over, because on the bottom was the mark, T. M. R. MADELEY, the initials being those of the founder of the factory, Thomas Martin Randall. As I write these words I still await an opportunity of taking photographs of this fine marked piece which, of course, will illustrate an article.

I find on reckoning up that I have written nearly five hundred articles about collecting, for six different magazines. I wonder what I found to talk about. Like every enthusiast, as I have said several times already, I like nothing better than to preach my gospel, but it is very easy to repeat what others have said before, probably in much better words. Every different editor has his own policy. One may be guided by a desire to instil canons of good taste into his readers, another may admire good craftsmanship, another may wish to lead the amateur on the right lines, and another may welcome new theories, however harebrained, and announce new discoveries. That is why the same pieces, or classes of pieces, may well provide the subject for many articles written in quite different vein. Then there are books to be reviewed, and that is not always a pleasant task, particularly when the author is an acquaintance. Who knows, he may in turn be asked to deal with one's own work at some future date! All the same, an honest review is the only one that is worth while, and if a book revives fallacies or suggests clear absurdities, or if its illustrations will not bear scrutiny with a magnifying glass, then the reading public must be told about it. But in fairness to an author, would it not be well if he were to be given an opportunity to answer his critics, in the pages of the same magazine? There is always anonymity, of course, but a reviewer who resorts to it is shirking his responsibilities. On the other hand, some editors, for various reasons, do prefer that a contributor should use a pseudonym. It may be that he is a dealer who, for some strange reason, is not always welcomed as a writer, or that it is inadvisable for articles on, say, ceramics and furniture to appear in the same number under the same name. In any case it is usually not long before the cat is out of the bag, for every writer has his own style, and that is a thing he cannot, and would not wish to change.

Ten

BUYING at auction can be a most satisfying way of making a collection. The very atmosphere of the sale-room, tense, combative, sometimes almost guilty, adds a certain glamour to the acquisition of a new piece. The longer the struggle, the keener the competition, the greater is the joy of possession if the price is right, as it will be only if the strange fever of the sale-room, the mad impulse to secure at all costs, can be resisted.

There are many different kinds of auctions. Consider first the ordinary country sale, where after a week's frenzied work, 'Tom' or 'George' has resolved an amazing variety of chattels into manageable and (unbelievable though it may seem) saleable lots. Tom (or George) may be recognized by his apron, and it is always well worth making his acquaintance. He can tell you at what time every lot will be put up; he knows pretty well what it will fetch, and if you cannot attend the sale in person he will bid for you. He knows much more about the contents of the house than the auctioneer, and he is a bit of a dealer himself. This kind of sale usually starts in the attic. It is most unlikely that all those who throng the tiny rooms and the steep, narrow staircase can possibly be interested in iron bedsteads and tin trunks, but thither they go like sheep at the first tinkle of the porter's bell, and thence to the downstairs rooms and corridors until, at last, they emerge thankfully into the fresh air to buy lawnmowers, garden seats, and Victorian knife-cleaners in the back-yard. Some, wiser or more disillusioned, find comfortable chairs close to the lots they have set their hearts on. At last, in comes the auctioneer with his clerk, the buzz of conversation dies down, and the first lot is put up.

'And now we come to Lot 136. This is what you've all been waiting for! Let's see, what is it? Ah, yes! An easy chair with patterned chintz loose covers and two down cushions. Where is it? George! George! There you are, George! Where's Lot 136? Ah! There it is over in the corner! Mr. Brown's sitting in it! Get up a minute, Mr. Brown, you can sit down again when it's sold! Hold it up, George! Give him a hand, sir, if you don't mind!' (George's head and shoulders disappear beneath the frill, and the chair is hoisted unsteadily aloft.)

'Now, there's a beautiful chair! Worth a tenner if it's worth a penny! Who'll start me with five pounds? Five pounds I'm bid! Five pounds! No? Well, who'll make me a bid? Come along, ladies and gentlemen, don't be shy! Ten bob, sir? Right, ten bob it is! Ten bob! Ten bob! Do I see fifteen by the window? Thank you, madam! Fifteen! Fifteen! Fifteen! Who'll make it a pound? One pound I am bid for this fine chair! The cushions alone are worth the money! Show 'em the cushions, George! Thank you, sir! One pound I am bid, then! Selling at one pound! Do I hear twenty-five? Twenty-five I'm bid! Thirty! That's better! Thirty! Thirty! Thirty shillings only I am bid. Going at thirty! I shall sell at thirty shillings! Two pounds! Two pounds! No, not you, madam! The bid is against you! Shall I say two pounds ten? Yes? Any advance on two pounds ten? Two pounds ten for a real antique! Lift up her skirts, George, and show the ladies and gentlemen her legs! H'mm! That doesn't matter, only wants a bit of glue! Fifty shillings! Again, sir? Fifty shillings, then, and I'm giving it away! Going at two pounds ten! Have you all done? Two pounds ten! Going! Going at two pounds ten! For the last time!' And down goes the hammer. And ten to one the lady was only scratching her nose, and he has to start all over again. No wonder that thirty lots in the hour is thought to be good going!

The dealers at this kind of sale usually huddle together in little groups. Every now and again one of them leaves on some mysterious errand in another room, in which case one notices that he always returns just in the nick of time to signal frantically to the auctioneer over the heads of the crowd in the doorway, just as his lot is put up. Their general aspect is one of utter despair. They don't know why on earth they ever came! Nothing there for any of them! Still, they always come, and what is more they bid eagerly, and look pityingly or with pretended amusement at the locals who oppose them.

Bidding at local auctions proceeds along certain fixed lines. On the whole it is vociferous as far as ordinary folk are concerned, who shout belligerently or apologetically, according to their nature. A few dealers do the same, glaring round as though no one else ought to bid at all, but the usual professional method is to give a quick upward jerk of the head, accompanied by a raising of the eyebrows and a sidelong glance at the auctioneer. It is a wonder they do not crick their necks. Dealers of better standing often bid with a flick of their catalogues or a lift of their pencils, and it is quite amazing to see how quickly a good auctioneer spots those who are in the bidding. The rest of his audience take good care to keep their heads and limbs perfectly still and to look in any direction other than that of his table or desk.

It is perfectly obvious that a very small proportion of a country sale audience really go to buy. Audience is indeed the right word; they go for entertainment and are usually not disappointed. They go too, of course, because a sale is their only chance to see the inside of the big house. A few weeks before they would not have dared to go near the front door, but now they muddy the carpets and paw over the furniture, the china, glass, and books as though the place belonged to them. A sale is a rare leveller.

At the other extreme are the world-famous sale-rooms of Sothebys and Christies. They are the magnets which attract the finest antiques in the world and the collectors and dealers who buy them. Just as the stud-book is the 'who's who' of a racehorse, so the history of a really rare specimen can be traced through the years by the frequency with which it has been described and illustrated in their catalogues.

I will describe, if I can, the conduct of a Sotheby sale. I say 'if I can' advisedly, because atmosphere is something that is not easily expressed in words. From the time that one enters the narrow entrance hall and climbs up the staircase to the lofty, well-lit galleries above, to the fall of the hammer at the last bid of the day, the bustle and roar of New Bond Street is left far behind. It is another world, a quiet world, a world in which attention is focused to the exclusion of all else on the treasures of a more gracious, less nerve-racking age. It is a world where beauty sets the pace and is understood, and where fortunes change hands like halfpence at a nod of the head and the giving of a name. A world, if you like, of gentlemen's agreements.

Goods for sale at these rooms can usually be viewed for several weeks in advance, from the time when catalogues have been published and sent out all over the world to those who subscribe for them. On the day of the sale they are still there, hanging on the walls, displayed in cabinets, or arranged on tables. At last a signal is given and the regulars take their places at a great U-shaped table inside which there is room for the porters to carry the more portable lots in their careful hands, or on their trays. The auctioneer mounts his rostrum, he adjusts his microphone, and without delay announces the first lot.

It is assumed that no one is present who is not a prospective buyer, and that everyone has a catalogue or at least does not need to hear the lots described. Accordingly, 'Lot 1,' says the auctioneer, 'a Pembroke table. What am I bid?' There is no cajolery, no imaginary bids, and no long pauses. Just the quiet, impassive voice accepting the bids until, when it is clear that the limit is reached, the hammer falls gently. When a particularly important lot is put up there is a stir of interest and the fringe of bidders behind the chairs presses a little forward, but the only sign that thousands of pounds, perhaps, have changed hands in the space of a few minutes is a buzz of excited conversation that dies away as the next lot is brought out. It is not surprising that eighty lots in the hour is commonplace.

Anyone who has attended an ordinary country sale—and who has not?—will have noticed what to the uninitiated is a most mysterious proceeding. At the end of the sale, and sometimes in the middle of it, a gaggle of dealers withdraws into a quiet corner of the garden. There they put their heads together, and there is a quiet murmur of conversation and sometimes the clink of money, after which the meeting disperses and back its members come into the house. Sometimes, too, the conversation is not so subdued. Voices are heard to be raised in anger, and I have known several occasions when a bleeding nose or a black eye has seemed to indicate that the proceedings did not pass off as amicably as might have been desired.

Such a meeting as this has to do with 'The Ring,' an illegal banding together of dealers the purpose of which is to obtain goods at low prices. I shall not presume, here, to pass any judgement upon its moral significance. Its existence has been both condemned and applauded, dependent on the point of view. Nevertheless, I will try to explain how it works, leaving my readers to draw their own conclusions.

Let us suppose that a particular lot, a fine piece of china, for example, is so obviously desirable that the trade is determined that it shall not fall into private hands. Clearly, there is money in it, if only it can be bought at the right price. Those who are members of the Ring, some of them locals but others outsiders who cannot be ignored, appoint one of their number to bid on their behalf, and the rest are silent. Unless a collector is determined and rich enough to buy at a price that puts any trade profit out of the question, the Ring's agent secures the piece. Then comes the huddle together or, on the other hand, it may be delayed until some time later in the day, perhaps over a table in the local inn. The lot is put up again and one dealer, who we will call Smith, makes the highest bid, a bid, mind, that is much nearer the true market value of the article than the price obtained by the auctioneer. Smith pays his money into the 'kitty,' the original bidder takes out the amount of his own bid, and whatever remains is divided equally among all the members, he and Smith included.

That, it might be supposed, is the end of the business. Not necessarily, by any means! However much Smith may wish to keep his prize he may well be a member of an inner, more exclusive Ring which holds another 'knock-out,' held on exactly the same lines. Dealers are, of course, very careful who they invite to 'Come in with us,' for the smaller the Ring the greater the share of the kitty for each of its members, some of which may go home well in pocket without having bought a single thing. They have been paid, in fact, for withholding their opposition.

The significance of the Ring, from the vendor's and the auctioneer's points of view, is that the former does not get a fair market price for his goods—the price, that is, that Smith had to pay—and the latter loses commission. The dealer, on the other hand, points out that his living depends on his being able to buy at low prices. He can say with some truth that after all he is the expert, or at least he professes to be, and that if anyone thinks a lot is worth more, and is willing to outbid the Ring, well, what is to stop him? Apart from the ethical pros and cons the Ring does, I think, introduce a nasty element into a profession that ought to be, and at best certainly is, far above the level of ordinary business. Furthermore, the endeavour to buy in the cheapest market and to sell in the dearest is more artificial than to buy openly against all bidders and to sell at a reasonable profit. Some dealers, for one reason or another, never join a Ring. They are usually those whose knowledge is such that they can afford to outbid it. I know of a case where at a London auction a piece started at 5s. At £21 someone said, 'Oh, he's not in the Ring but he's not a bad fellow. Let him have it now we've made him pay through the nose!' As he left the room with the piece under his arm, having paid cash on the spot, a dealer said, 'And what d'ye think you've got there?' The answer came pat. 'I don't have to think, I know!' So he did, for the same afternoon he sold it for £250! Sometimes the Ring does know that a piece is really valuable, and those outside it have a fight on their hands. It was the same abstainer who at Christies had an open commission to buy a certain piece. The lot started at 50 guineas. When it had reached the record figure of 10,000 guineas the rich client walked over to his agent. 'Whose was that bid?' he whispered. 'Yours!' was the reply. Rich as he was he very nearly fainted. 'For God's sake, be quiet!' he hissed. Then, just as the hammer was about to fall, the great Duveen nodded his head! 'Thank God!' said the client, faintly. And be sure his agent echoed his words! A rich collector or a knowledgeable dealer can be a friend indeed to the owner of a fine piece that is put up for auction. Some years ago a fine Toby was offered at Christies, with a reserve of £70. The Ring dropped out at £200, and the owner, who was present, was rubbing his hands. Imagine his surprise when the fight continued between a dealer and a collector, and his delight when the former won at a record figure of no less than £650!

Cases are not unknown in which a dealer who does not play fair with his colleagues is taught a sharp lesson. Rohan tells the story of one who, years ago, earned their enmity by refusing to part with certain pieces he had bought on their behalf. They bided their time. Then, at last, he was chosen to bid, for the Ring as he thought, for a most expensive piece. Of course, he secured it, but when the time came for the knock-out he was told that as he had bought the piece he might keep it, as far as they were concerned. There was nothing he could do. He was ruined, and died shortly afterwards.

It may well be asked why, if the activities of the Ring are forbidden by law, can they not be prevented? Surely a law that cannot be enforced must be a bad one? The truth is that the police are powerless to interfere. The huddle in the garden, in the village inn, or in a London sale-room could be interrupted, but what proof would there be of law-breaking? Besides, it could be resumed later on. That is the position. The remedy, from the collector's point of view, is that he must decide what he is prepared to pay for a coveted piece. He may then bid up to that figure in the knowledge that if his assessment of its value is correct he will outbid the Ring, for its members have an eye not only to its ultimate selling price, but to their share of the kitty.

A really important country sale is, of course, the dealers' field day, and it is a sign of the times that so many great houses and estates have become such a burden on their owners that they are having to be sold. It is difficult to understand why as a nation we countenance and even enforce what is surely an impoverishment of our heritage. It is obviously true that death duties help the national exchequer—though before long the source must inevitably dry up—but on the other side of the balance sheet it has apparently been forgotten that, apart from the fact that a great country estate is a part of an England many of us love, its existence provided employment for every man and woman for miles around. Moreover, it was on the whole happy employment, for those who lived under the protection of the great house were surely as secure as and certainly more contented than the harassed creatures of a welfare state. A beneficent autocracy has a great deal to be said for it.

As a young lad I spent many happy days fishing in the great pools a stone's throw from the pillared terraces of such a country mansion. My companion was the son of the estate manager, and when the noble owner was away from home we crept fearfully past the great fountains to peer through the staring, empty windows at the treasures inside. Sometimes we climbed swaying ladders, towering into the darkness, to where beneath a golden dome a great bell terrified us with its sudden clangour as it struck the hour. Beneath, on every side, a petrified forest of chimney-stack, slate, and cat-walk. But when the Earl was in residence everything was changed indeed! The vast gardens were quickly immaculate under the skilled care of forty pairs of hands, the cavernous corridor in the basement, 10 feet wide and nearly 100 yards long, echoed unceasingly to the quick traffic of countless hurrying, busy feet, and outside, in the sunshine, a roar like thunder and a sudden fierce jet of sparkling, triumphant water, 150 feet in height, paid tribute to the labours of the chief engineer and his staff in an engine-room from whose tiled floor one could have enjoyed a meal. And every day the fire-brigade rehearsed a duty they hoped never to have to perform in real earnest, and their master, when the fancy took him, travelled to London by special train.

Such a regime could not last. It so happened that a factory worker from a nearby town was a member of a party that had been invited to visit the lovely grounds, and it is said that as he looked around him at so much beauty he said to a companion, 'Some day I will own all this!' His time came. The 1914–18 war gave him his opportunity, which he took with both capable hands. He became a millionaire, and he was knighted for his services to industry. So, in due course, one half of one of his millions was given in exchange for his heart's desire, and the new squire moved in.

Of all this I knew nothing when I was appointed the young headmaster of the school in the little village which I had known so well as a boy. I knew only that at the Court lived a baronet whom no one liked. He kept himself aloof and took no part in village affairs, though strangely enough, when he first came, he had been willing to do so. Worst of all, he was lacking in respect to the local Personalities! I was told that on one occasion a churchwarden, a retired Indian civil servant, had cause to request Sir James, as we will call him, to attend to the roof of the village church, which was part of the Court. No doubt he did not choose his words as well as he might have done, for despite the presence of the Rector the only answer he got was, 'You get off my b——y land!' I think the church was Sir James's sore point, because he had been heard to complain, 'The finest room in the whole house, and they wouldn't let me buy it!'

With such stories as these in my mind I thought I knew what to expect, though I thought it strange that every Christmas, without fail, a van came to the school from the Court laden with oranges, coconuts, and toys for the children, and chocolates and cigars for the staff. At least, so I was told. On the other hand, I knew that it had been the custom for the late headmaster to provide beaters for pheasant shooting, on any day of the week, and this honoured but quite illegal custom I had no intention of continuing. Sure enough, in due course a letter arrived, asking that a dozen boys might be permitted to appear at the Court, for beating purposes, on a Tuesday morning. I wrote politely enough, saying that such leave of absence was not in my power to grant. So much I thought, for the cigars and nuts!

Then, a week or two later (I think it was early summer), I circularized the villagers asking for contributions towards the cost of sports equipment. Should I send one to Sir James? Nothing venture, nothing win. I did so, not expecting a reply. To my surprise back came a prompt letter, inviting me to go to the Court at eight o'clock the following evening. I was there on the dot, and the butler led the way along wide corridors and through lovely, luxuriously furnished rooms to his master's study. Sir James was fishing, but if I would please wait he was not expected to be long.

I sat there for perhaps half an hour, and everything was quiet as the grave. Outside, beyond the courtyard, a herd of red deer grazed contentedly, and every now and again one of them would peer curiously through the bars of the great iron gates.

At last I heard soft footsteps approaching the door, which was flung open as Sir James rushed in. He was a short, fat man, quite bald, with no neck to speak of, in full evening dress. His eyes were small, rather piggish but very shrewd, and I noticed that his ringed hands were very white and carefully manicured. He apologized for his lateness, and said he had been fishing in the lake. I said that I, too, was fond of fishing, and he replied that as a rule he fished for salmon. With a fly-rod, I ventured to suppose?

'Fly-rod my foot!' was the astonishing reply. 'Too slow for me. I fishes for 'em with a trawl!'

And so he did, for I learnt later that he had a sea-going boat that he kept in an estuary in North Wales.

He sat down behind his big desk, signalled me to draw up a chair, and took out my circular from a drawer.

'Now, what's all this about?' he demanded. I told him of my intentions, and he made me tell him exactly what I wanted to buy.

He thought for a moment. Then he tossed the circular into a waste-paper basket.

'I tell you what to do. Get what you can out of these jacks-in-office, and let me know how much more you still want!'

I tried to stammer my thanks, but he cut me short. We talked about the school for a few minutes, then he suddenly asked, 'And what is a young fellow like you doing in a dead-alive place like this?' I explained that one had to make a start somewhere, and he grunted. Then, 'If I was a young chap like you, you wouldn't see my bottom for dust!' Only, he didn't say 'bottom'!

That was the first of many talks, and I soon found that there was hardly any topic about which he could not argue convincingly. His brain was as cold as ice, and I could see how he had made his millions. I could see, too, why he was so unpopular in the village. He had come with the best intentions, fully prepared to do all he could to help in every possible way. Unfortunately, the upper stratum of village social life would have none of it; they could not forget or forgive his lowly origin, and of course the cottagers followed their example. The result was that only the schoolchildren and their teachers benefited by the generosity he had been prepared to extend to all. One other exception he made. Let him hear only that some old fellow was sick and neglected, and off he would go, in any weather, to take hot food and other comforts. Very few knew about this side of his complex character.

One night, when my wife and I had been in bed for some hours, we were awakened by loud voices and the noise of cars and motorcycles in the road outside. I got out of bed and looked through the window, to see the sky ablaze with red light. 'The Court's on fire!' I exclaimed, and we dressed quickly, got out my car, and drove along the road to a place from where we had a clear view. True enough, the entire front, the great pillared portico between the two square towers, was studded with squares of orange-red, and as we watched, from the pinnacled tops of the towers themselves streamers of black smoke writhed into the angry sky, to give place, in an instant it seemed, to twisting tongues of yellow flame. And every few minutes, above the roar of the fire, we could hear the thunder of collapsing floors, and see the sudden, swift fountains of sparks shooting up into the sky. Any fire of such magnitude is at once a magnificent and a terrifying sight, but I could think only of the many treasures that were feeding the flames, and we did not stay. Later, we heard that Sir James had been on the South Coast when the news was telephoned to him, and that he had driven through the night in his Rolls at breakneck speed, only to arrive when all that remained of the finest part of his home, the state rooms, was a smoking ruin.

Of course, there had been willing helpers, and a great deal of valuable furniture was saved. One local man cut himself badly by walking straight through a plate-glass window. It was rumoured that there was some looting, and that several fine pairs of silver candlesticks had appeared suddenly on the market. Fortunately, the wonderful church was spared, and only a few weeks ago it was announced that public funds had been granted towards its restoration. As to the rest, the blackened ruins still stand in the centre of the great park, and grass grows on the terraces which were trod by Queen Adelaide and, within living memory, by King Edward VII.

Enough furniture had been salvaged to make up a sale which attracted dealers from all over the country, and the view-days afforded an opportunity for the villagers to explore what remained of the stately house they had previously only admired from the church drive. They turned out in their Sunday best, as if to pay respect, and for the first time I heard good things said about Sir James. My wife and I walked down the long drive, and took the right fork at the church, to enter what seemed to be the deserted streets of a small town. Stables, workshops, coach-houses, and store-rooms, with here and there a cottage to complete the illusion, until at length we reached the entrance to that great main corridor along which a coach and horses could have been driven and which ended in a tiny semicircle of light far away in the distance. It was strange to find comfortable living quarters down there in the gloom, the servants' hall, the housekeeper's room, and the butler's pantry, and to see the spacious meat stores, still-rooms, and pantries which gave mute evidence of a way of life that has gone.

We mounted a wide stone-flagged staircase and walked along an echoing, dim corridor to the main entrance hall. So far there was no sign of the fire. Then, suddenly, we looked up at the blue sky through a network of charred rafters, and had perforce to pick our way carefully through the blackened debris and shattered glass that littered the once white marble floor. I turned over with my toe a fragment of crimson carpet. I remembered that not so long ago I had crossed that same carpet to the foot of the staircase, and that the butler had glared reprovingly at a servant who had paused from her dusting to watch our passage. The staircase was still there, winding gracefully to the gallery that had once been decked with cabinets of buhl and satinwood, and my eye followed its course to where, high above, a great steel tank, its sides twisted and warped, still rested upon steel girders. All this would not have happened, I thought, if Sir James had kept the fire-brigade.

The auction sale was held in a great marquee, and it was noticeable that the dealers were outnumbered by private buyers from other country houses. There were many strangers, amongst them Mrs. Van der Elst, who sat unmoving, white-faced and clothed in black from head to foot, while her secretary, I suppose he was, bid for piece after piece of graceful, ornate French furniture. What a great deal of brass there was! Scores of saucepans, sets of jelly-moulds, and skillets by the dozen. They went for a song. The Rector bought the first of innumerable over-stuffed arm-chairs for £2 10s. 0d., and all the others fetched three or four times as much. And I was so taken by surprise when the bidding on a Georgian chess-table lagged at a sovereign that I lost my chance of a bargain.

What is to be done with these great mansions? The fate of this one, at least, was determined by a careless kitchen-maid who let a pan of fat boil over on a kitchen range. Or so it was said. The collector, at least, can rejoice that he is at liberty to see beautiful and priceless treasures in their proper setting when others are thrown open to the public. The world and his wife can roam the lovely park at Longleat without having even heard of Capability Brown. He can admire its wonderful ceilings and furnishings, and stroll beside its fishponds. He can live for a space in the Golden Age, and—who knows?—he may even realize that there are other things worth while than football pools and the late sports finals.

Some time ago, more out of curiosity than anything else, we went to a view-day, preparatory to a four days' sale. We parked our car in a field, with perhaps a hundred others, at the end of a long, shrub-lined drive. The house itself, gracious, seemingly asleep in the drowsy heat of a summer's afternoon, seemed to defy the centuries, although of no great age. But just inside the doorway, dispelling all illusion, a gipsy type of dealer sprawled in a Chippendale chair. As a collector I ought to have felt glad that so much furniture and fine china, so many pictures, even a complete staircase, would soon appear on the market, but I could feel nothing but sadness at their imminent dispersal. The following evening the sale was featured on television, the first time, I suppose, such a thing had ever been done. The auctioneer spoke of the difficulties of cataloguing the contents of such a place, and hinted at the excitement of finding, for instance, the remainder of a set of Sheraton chairs in a lumber-room. He spoke also of the Ring, and to my surprise he seemed to approve of its activities. Indeed, ignoring what I believe to be the legal aspect, he stressed the fact that in his opinion its existence would result in higher prices, since it is the dealers who make a sale and who are prepared to buy, and since private buyers, lacking knowledge, are afraid to pay high prices. There is much in what he said, but I cannot believe that if the Ring was abolished the dealers would stay away. After all, they must attend sales if they are to stay in business, and they would still pay the same prices, with the difference that the money would go to the vendor and not into the kitty. It is as simple as that.

Many pieces bought at auction are sent to America. Of recent years, since the last war during which so many Americans were able to study our way of life and to see at first hand the wonders of our heritage of craftsmanship, the flow has been ever-increasing. Apart from the 'recent shipment from Europe' that is a feature of advertisement in the American journals, dealers come across every year, and though at first inferior Victorian bric-à-brac was attractive to a young country with few antiques of her own, times have changed, and much that is irreplaceable is leaving us for ever. The well-known story of the G.I. who, seeing 'Lot 48' chalked on an arm-chair took that figure to be the price in dollars, would no longer ring true! Americans are beginning to understand and to use their own judgement, and prices in their auction rooms tend to be high if the goods are fine. In the early days, at any rate, there was a good deal of showmanship. Sales were held after dinner, and the buyers attended in tuxedos. Nothing was on show in the sale-room, but at one end there was a brightly-lit stage at the side of which, in front of the curtain, was the auctioneer's rostrum. The lot number was called out, up went the curtain, and there was the piece on a table, looking ten times worth its true value.

Many unscrupulous dealers doubtless took advantage of transatlantic ignorance to foist wrong pieces on American buyers, but even the most knowledgeable collector among us must confess that at some time or another he has bought a 'fake.' A book has been written about them, which indicates that they are numerous enough to constitute a very real danger. It is something of a comfort, however, to remember that the fake of a really valuable piece costs a great deal to make, so that it, as well as its original, may well be out of reach. On the other hand, many craftsmen and factories have imitated old china, furniture, and glass simply because they were worth imitating. These copies were sold for what they were, honestly, at fair prices, but the position is altogether changed when they are re-sold at a later date. As an example, imitations of Sheraton and Hepplewhite furniture were made at the time of the Great Exhibition, imitations so good, so well-made, that they pass nowadays for the genuine article. They are every bit as good, but they are not 'right'. A friend of mine commissioned a cabinet-maker, a few years ago, to make for him a writing-desk of well-seasoned walnut, in the Queen Anne style. It is so true to period, so lovely and well-proportioned, that some day it will be accepted as what it is not, and was never intended to be.

Consistent with the emphasis that has been the theme of the previous chapters I think I ought to say a little about the main classes of ceramic fakes that the collector is most likely to meet. No English porcelain has been so imitated as Worcester of the early period. It is not necessary to try to copy the paste and glaze, because there is an abundance of ware painted with simple underglaze blue patterns to which more elaborate decoration can be applied. Careful examination and experience are needed to combat this kind of fake; signs of re-firing, traces of blue peeping out from under the borders of claret or apple-green, and incongruous combinations of different styles are among the clues for which the expert seeks. Samson of Paris made wonderful copies of Worcester; wonderful, that is, from the decorative point of view, although his paste was always 'hard,' and his square-marks pale and underglaze, instead of overglaze, and indigo in colour. His 'Chelsea' often bears enormous gold anchors, and his 'Derby' figures have crossed batons and D's in the wrong places. Make no mistake, however. One day in the not too far-distant future Samson's wares will be valuable in their own right, and some museums, Swansea among them, have already begun to put them on show.

It should not be supposed that ordinary 'blue and white' is always safe to buy. Booths of Tunstall copied some of the well-known Worcester printed patterns, such as the 'pine-cone,' on earthenware, and so did another firm whose mark was a CB monogram that is not listed in the marks books. On the other hand, one can be too careful! When I first began to collect I thought I knew the difference between porcelain and pottery. The one was opaque, and the other was translucent, or so I believed. With this rule of thumb in mind I carefully examined a pair of large leaf-shaped dishes or trays that I had bought by poor light from Julius Brookes, of Birmingham. He sold them to me as Bow. To my horror, when I held each piece in turn against a strong electric lamp, they were perfectly opaque! I had been had! Back they went, and I brought away something else, I forget what it was, in exchange. Not until much later, when it was too late, did I discover that much early Bow is indeed opaque, and that I had missed two very good pieces. Of course, I ought to have known they were much too heavy for earthenware.

Beware of Coalport 'goat and bee' jugs that pretend to be early Chelsea. Rose was very proud of the white, wonderfully translucent paste that Billingsley had taught him to make, and he often tried to see what he could do with it. In this connection a friend of mine, Franklin Barrett of Derby, visited the present Coalport works in the Potteries to examine the old copper engraved plates, prints from some of which were published in his book on the Salopian porcelains. He found a cellar-full, although several tons, he was told, had been melted down during the war for salvage. He spent a filthy, sweaty day down there in the gloom, and among the plates he came across the original ones that had evidently been used to print a SWANSEA mark on Coalport porcelain. It would appear that an occasional piece of 'Swansea' may not be all it pretends to be!

Of recent years prices of early Staffordshire pottery have risen by leaps and bounds, and excellent imitations have been made in Spain and Portugal. Many are so good that they have found places in well-known collections—dare I quote the case of the auctioned Toby jug? Whatever is in fashion is bound to be imitated. Copper lustre was not always the glut on the market that it is at the moment. A few years ago it was possible to buy it by the crate at a few pence per piece, every piece literally fire-new. I do not know whether the valuable silver-resist pieces have ever been copied, but I fancy not. In fact, I was told a few weeks ago by the manager of a modern pottery that at long last his chemists were on the verge of inventing a silver lustre that would have some of the mellow characteristics of the old.

When I was last in the Swansea district I was shown what must be one of the finest collections of Swansea and Nantgarw porcelain in this country. The brightly-lit cabinets resembled nothing so much as miniature English flower-gardens. The proud owner of all this beauty picked up a saucer, wonderfully painted with birds. 'See if you can find the repair!' he said. I examined it most carefully with a glass, but could find nothing amiss. Only when I held it against the light did a darker transparency reveal the fact that a large crescent-shaped piece had been inserted into the rim, painted, and glazed. If the piece had been opaque I could never have known that it was other than perfect. That was, indeed, the position as regards 'made-up' pottery until a short time ago. Then came the advent of the ultra-violet lamp.

I know that my Staffordshire pottery-collecting friend had tried to obtain one of these lamps for some time. It seemed almost as though there were a conspiracy to keep them out of the hands of collectors, though we had heard of several dealers who possessed one. At last, by dint of judicious string-pulling, he was more fortunate, and I went to see how it was used. When I arrived there it was on a low table, and under it was a small Whieldon figure of a Chinese boy. This was a recent addition to the collection, an impish, laughing little fellow, as naked and unashamed as the day he was born, a copy of a Chinese original, and apparently quite perfect in every detail. The room lighting was switched off, and the lamp switched on. Immediately the figure glowed with an intense purple light, but around the neck we could see a thin white line, and one hand and both feet stood out in the same sharp contrast in the same chalky colour. Even the brush-marks, getting thinner as the colour of the new pigment smoothed into the old, were clearly visible. And yet, when the lamp was switched off, and knowing just where to look, we could see no sign of the repairs. We went through the entire collection, and found several made-up pieces. One fine Ralph Wood Toby had been given a complete new hat, but no one would have known it, for the paste and the coloured glaze passed every ordinary test. I do not pretend to explain why any kind of repair should show up white under the lamp, but it is obvious that this new invention will be a boon to dealers and collectors alike, for there cannot be any doubt that many perfect pieces, perfect that is by ordinary standards, are not what they seem. Why else do badly damaged Bow and Chelsea figures command high prices at auction?

There are degrees of excellence where restorations are concerned. The Toby had been properly done, real clay had been used, and it and the covering glaze had been fired in a kiln. I once bought a pair of Dresden candelabra from which several sconces were missing, and had new ones made and fixed by a specialist repairer. These were made of fired porcelain, and the only mistake was that the shrinkage had been slightly miscalculated, so that the new parts were just a shade too small. Lower down the scale are repairs made of some kind of plaster, coloured with oil or water-colours, and varnished. These are comparatively easy to detect. The paste does not ring clear, and the 'glazed' surface is not properly smooth and clean to the touch. If the repair is recent one can even smell the paint, which can easily be removed with a knife. But what is even more important, the chinese-white that is used for the undecorated parts and for flesh tints yellows with age. As an example of this, I once attended a sale to buy a picture in which I was interested. As I waited the porter carried in a large Capo di Monti group of three goddesses, finely modelled and coloured, but one of the ladies had lost an arm. No one was very interested, and I secured it for 5s. I lost no time in sending it away to be repaired, and in the course of a few weeks back it came, as good as new, at a cost of 30s. I told a friend, a 'private dealer,' about the repair, and he was glad to buy the piece for £4 10s. 0d. He, in turn, passed it on to another dealer for £10, and before very long there it was in his window marked £17 10s. 0d.! Every time I passed by there it still was. But, as I fully expected, every time the new arm was always just a little yellower until, within a year, it stood out like a sore thumb! Five shillings was about its proper price.

A reputable dealer does not sell anything without declaring a known repair or restoration, and a collector will sometimes buy a piece so defective until such time as he can find a perfect one. There is no harm in the owner of a damaged specimen attempting a repair in order to make it more presentable in his cabinet, and such ready-mixed compositions as 'Joystixin' can be used, with practice and a little patience, to produce quite professional results. A most effective and durable body, especially for pottery, can be made from a mixture of dental plaster of Paris and some adhesive such as 'Certofix' or 'Seccotine,' which sets very hard and can then be filed or sandpapered. If it is necessary to make up the broken rim of a plate, for instance, it is best to stick a piece of gummed paper on the underside to support the mixture, peeling it off when it is properly set. Arms and legs can be built up, layer by layer, on a match-stick or wire 'skeleton.' The secret is never to try to do too much at once, for the inside of a really thick mass of mixture never properly sets. Decoration is best done with water-colour and clear picture-varnish. Repairs of this kind to porcelain can easily be detected because they are opaque, but brown-glazed earthenware is particularly easy to repair because there is no need to use chinese-white, and there is never any later discoloration.

Enough, then, of repairs and restorations. Forget fakes for a moment, even though they are always with us. In a collector's Utopia there would be no place for them, and his cabinets would be filled with perfect pieces, every one a rarity and every one displayed to the best advantage. Utopia or not, the question of proper display, and of all that goes with it, contributes a great deal to the pride and joy of possession. The search at an end, the gloating over and done with, the collector, as my wife puts it, 'must play with his toys.' Here, then, are some practical suggestions.

Confining my remarks to ceramics I ought first to repeat what I have already said, that fine pieces may either be used for their originally intended purposes, or else be displayed in cabinets or upon open shelves. In the first regard no one, unless possessed of considerable wealth or devoid of proper respect for age and beauty, would take tea from a Worcester tea-service painted with exotic birds and scale-blue. On the other hand, a great bowl of 'Chinese Lowestoft,' filled with flowers, enriches the humblest side-table, and can come to small harm. A pair of Spode or Minton vases looks better on a mantelpiece than in a cabinet, since their form and decoration can brook no detracting rivals, and it is no great sin to put a colourful Mason's Ironstone or Coalport foot-bath to alien use by filling it with bulbs. Good china, properly positioned, enhances any and every room, but common sense must govern one's choice of pieces. For myself, I value my possessions enough to insist that they be displayed behind glass, avoiding any resemblance to a museum by careful choice of cabinets. A private house is no place for a plate-glass showcase. Nevertheless, if I ever made a collection, say, of any sort of comparatively cheap earthenware, I should try to set it out on open shelves, preferably in a room to itself.

Cabinet arrangement is to a large extent a matter of personal taste, but there are certain rules which ought to be obeyed if ugliness is to be avoided. Blue and white does not live happily with polychrome wares, and neither, as a rule, should Chinese 'Blue Nankin' be placed near to the English 'soft paste' blue-painted or blue-printed porcelains. Similarly, blue-printed earthenware is not intended for cabinet display, and in any case must be kept to itself.

Owen Wheeler once expounded a theory to me that is perhaps worth passing on. He drew two moon-like faces on a piece of paper. In one of them he made the eyebrows and mouth quirk up at the corners, but in the other they were made to droop down.

'Now,' said he, 'which is cheerful, and which is glum?' Of course, it was obvious. 'All right, then,' he went on, 'always arrange the pieces on a mantelpiece or on a cabinet shelf low in the centre and high at the sides.'

Cabinets should be electrically lighted, and the lighting should, if possible, be controlled by wall-switches. It is most effective to be able to illuminate all your treasures as you enter the room. If possible, too, use small striplights that can be tucked away out of sight so that they shine on the pieces and not into the eyes. Fluorescent lamps, or indeed strong light of any kind, should not be used; they are inimical to colours that were intended to be seen by candlelight.

Every collection, no matter how small, should be properly catalogued, and in order to do this each piece must be labelled. Small, plain, round labels, ready gummed, are quite suitable, but special ones printed with one's name are cheap enough to buy and add a certain cachet to one's possessions. Some collectors even have printed factory names as well, which is all very well if one collects only several kinds of ware, but almost impossible if one's tastes are catholic. And in this connection the labels of former owners should never be removed, since they afford an interesting history of the piece which bears them. How about washing? The remedy is quite simple. Cover each label with a thin coat of transparent varnish ('Cellure' is admirable) and it will never wash off.

First, then, each piece must bear a label of some kind, the smaller the better, bearing a number. Pieces belonging to each other, say a tea-pot and its lid and stand, bear the same number. This is the catalogue reference, and against it are entered the following particulars: nature of the piece, full detailed description, size, date, factory or place of origin, history if known, similar pieces in known collections or featured in books of reference, mark, where purchased, and price paid. Apart from the enjoyment gained from making a catalogue of this kind, it is of the utmost value at such time as the collection has to be sold.

The possessor of a suitable camera should try to photograph every piece. Large prints may then be mounted in a separate album, and smaller ones may be fixed in the catalogue. When I first began to collect blue and white I found it convenient to use for this purpose the tiny prints which I cut from old pages of the *Connoisseur*. Otherwise, I made small pen and ink sketches which served the same purpose.

All this takes time, but it is a labour of love. At least it affords an excuse to haunt one's cabinets!

I am very near to the end of my story, and yet I wonder whether I have really done what I set out to do? I have tried to express some of the joys, the disappointments, and the adventures that are a part of this fascinating business of collecting. I have passed on, perhaps, a little practical knowledge that has come of experience. But now, as I reach for the last sheet of foolscap, I know that perhaps I have been more fortunate than the average present-day collector can ever hope to be. I began just in time to see what must have been the end of the vintage collecting years, when every dealer was something of a connoisseur who loved the things he had to sell, when antiques were plentiful and cheap because they were not fully understood and rarely appreciated by the layman, and when a wide world of discovery lay before the chosen few who had eyes to see and the will to understand. I have said a great deal about those who taught me so willingly and whose experiences I shared, and it comes as somewhat of a shock when I realize that they have passed on, and that others of my age may have come quite unconsciously to stand in the same relationship to young collectors who will follow after us.

Truly, we collectors are quite incorrigible! No sooner have I laid down my pen than, before the ink is dry, I shall be hastening to my cabinets to look again at my two latest pieces of Mason's Ironstone China, which I have begun to collect simply because in a junk-shop (where I thought I was safe!) I happened to see a tall beaker so well-painted that I took it to be Chinese porcelain of fine quality. There is indeed no cure for the bite of the collecting bug. We may have spent our last shilling on some beautiful trifle, and our suits may be frayed and out at the elbows. We may be the despair of our bank managers and the heavy cross of our wives. But, counting what in our hearts we know to be our blessings, which of us would have it otherwise?

Eleven

SINCE I finished writing the last chapter thirteen years have gone by. I remember that I heaved a sigh of relief, sat back, and awaited the consequences. I was lucky. None of my friends resented what I had said about them, and it was not long before I had made many new ones. Letters came in from foreign parts—a delightful one from Owen Wheeler's daughter among them—and I was again and again reminded of many forgotten incidents. And I was glad above all, though perhaps I felt just a little guilty, to know that my book had led quite a number of hitherto happy innocents into the insidious paths of collecting.

A great deal has happened since then. The sharer of my love for blue and white, Derek Cooper, has passed on, not so long ago. His treasure house of lovely furniture, porcelain, clocks and pictures has been dispersed, and I am often sad to realize that I shall never again gossip with him under the great cedars on a summer's evening. And what a surprise it would be to him if he could know the value that was placed by some younger collector on his favourite Bow shaving-mug!

Twelve years ago I left the classroom (with a six years' interruption in a steel works) to become an antique dealer on a capital of £450. It was possible then, and I had many advantages. Like all collectors who sometimes have to sell in order to buy I had already done some dealing, and was on friendly terms with the local trade. Even though I was a 'bloody schoolmaster.' I was fairly well known through my several books and my hundreds of articles in the collecting magazines, and above all I found a good friend. Hamish Wolf (or Henry as he is usually called in the trade) had come over from his native Czecho-Slovakia during the war, and was now more English than the English. He took me under his wing. Every morning at half-past eight I left my car at his shop, and off we would go in his Austin. Sometimes we would cover as many as half a dozen sales in the day, viewing some, leaving prices at others, and staying on if it seemed promising. Usually, somewhere on the way, we picked up Bert. Now, Bert was a sprightly 70-year-old then, one of the old school of dealers who could smell a 'right' piece of furniture across the width of a marquee. If we stayed on, most of us perched ourselves on a convenient table or chest of drawers somewhere in the background, but not Bert. He stood up all day like a little, wise old owl in a trilby, and never seemed to tire. His death a few months ago will leave an unfillable gap. I never see a Lyons fruit tart without thinking of those sale days, because such was our staple diet at the transport cafés on the long jaunt home. Or a Wimpey's hamburger. In those days, and before I was elected a member of B.A.D.A. in 1962, we 'settled' and until I saw it I never would have believed that a couple of dozen large men could squeeze into a pigsty. Sometimes we had more salubrious quarters, a back room perhaps, or the snug in a pub a few miles away, or even a corner of the garden if the day were fine, with Ronnie munching an apple he had picked from a tree. He was a Spartan character who wore an open-necked shirt with short sleeves on the coldest winter's day, and would have made a fortune as an artist, for the margins of his catalogue were always filled with lovely little sketches of the goods on offer. Sometimes, at a big sale with as many as two hundred dealers present, it might be eight or nine o'clock before we started home—one famous settlement dragged on until after two in the morning. As for the Ring itself, the less said the better. Except that, provided the owners of goods up for sale have them properly valued or that auctioneers make a point of paying experts to do it for them, very little harm can be done to anyone. That is the real answer, for no laws can ever stop what is virtually a dealers' self-defence organization. One old dealer once said to me, 'Talk about us dealers being crooks, you wait until you go to buy something privately, then you'll see who're the bloody crooks!' Just a little exaggerated, to say the least, but how often does the conversation go something like this: 'Can you tell me what sort of value you place on this piece?' 'Oh, I've no idea at all, can't you make me an offer?' 'Well' (making a fair offer to allow for a sensible profit), 'I can give you so-and-so.' 'Oh, I thought it would be worth about double that!' No idea of its value?

The free valuation trick is well known. At least to the trade. Mr. A., the owner, asks Mr. B., the dealer, to visit him to make an offer for some things he has for sale. Mr. B. travels miles to see them, and makes a fair offer. Half of the stuff, perhaps, he doesn't want as a gift, but there are several nice bits he could do with. 'Well, that seems very fair,' says Mr. A., all honest and smiling, 'but I'll have to ask my wife (or my father, or my second cousin) and if she agrees we'll let you know.' Mr. B. departs, knowing that he has had a wasted journey. Mr. A. thereupon calls in another dealer. 'I've been offered so much for this,' says he, 'but you can have it if you can do a bit better.' And so on through the alphabet. Well, it's every man's right to do the best he can for himself, but if Mr. B. asks a valuation fee, which he has every right to do, and indeed should do to protect himself, what a long face is pulled by Mr. A.!

The real villains in the Ring are the hangers-on. Usually they have no shops. The last thing they want is to buy anything to take away, and if by misadventure (or by low cunning on the part of the rest of the dealers) they are landed with any article their whole day is ruined, and the rest of their week is spent in hawking it round the trade to try to get their money back. Their method of operation is simple. Suppose a porcelain specialist, who knows his stuff, buys a good piece. In the settlement itself, keeping mum, the hanger-on gets his share of the 'kitty' with the rest. Then, after the business is done, up he goes to the final purchaser. 'I'm interested in that mug you bought. I'll put half a crown on it.' 'Five bob.' 'Seven and six.' 'Ten bob.' 'That's enough for me, I'll take the money.' And off he goes to find another victim, with ten shillings in his pocket towards his day's wages. Some dealers have seen the light, and only settle with those who understand and really want the goods, at the risk of unpopularity. But of course all these proceedings are really a myth, and never really happen.

To attend sales is the only way to learn the business, and I got to know some very interesting characters. Tommy Wyatt, whom I mentioned early in this book, was still flourishing, and long after he had to give up driving he still attended every sale to which he could get a lift. He died last year, still in harness, and the trade is the poorer for his passing. He would be the first to laugh at the affair of his cannons. These two enormous weapons stood at either side of his front gates, and he was very proud of them. One night they disappeared. For months afterwards everyone was greeted with the same remark. 'Did you hear how some b—— pinched my cannons?' Heart failure is an occupational hazard among dealers, and no wonder. One of Tommy's contemporaries called on me a few months ago. He had his son with him, driving the shooting brake with a roof-rack on top, and they bought a very large and heavy oak coffer. It must have weighed two or three hundredweights. I asked, would his man be calling for it? 'We'll take it with us,' he said. His son bent down to pick up one end, and I did the same at the other. The old man pushed me to one side. 'I'll do it, I'm more used to it than you!' And up it went, out through the door, and up on the rack as if it were a feather. I'd never have believed it. Only one thing daunts these old-stagers—present-day prices. The same dealer said to me one day, having just bought a rather nice sofa-table from me for £350, 'I don't know what things are coming to. D'ye know, when I was a lad and went with my father to Ireland to buy goods we always reckoned to buy a sofa-table or two. But it had to be a damn good 'un for him to give a fiver for it!'

I well remember one old Gloucestershire dealer who used to buy most of his furniture at Sothebys, but occasionally he did attend a local sale. When he did so he was always chairman at the settlement, as courtesy demanded. He used to sit at the head of the table like a carved image, glaring sternly round at the company. No pigsties for him. If he saw a strange face—'I don't know you! Does anybody know him? Has he got a shop?' And if he hadn't, then out he went. He travelled to sales in a Rolls-Royce, which was very fine until the Inland Revenue wondered whence he got the money to pay for it. Thereafter they made his life a misery.

The roof-rack was a wonderful invention, though car designers would be horrified and quite unbelieving if they knew how much weight antique dealers pile on. I called to see a friend one day to see a Worcester tankard he had found, but he was out, and expected every minute. I could not wait, and set off for home. Now, the road from his shop to my main road is a series of dips between very bad humpbacked bridges. As I approached one of these dips I saw what appeared to be the legs of an upturned table rising steadily upwards, to be followed by a dresser base piled on top of two chests of drawers. And this was merely the front layer, as it were. The height of the pile must have been all of ten feet, and how my friend had loaded, or how he unloaded, remains a mystery, for he would not let me help him, and I left him to it. A low railway bridge has seen the splintering of many a good piece, and I remember a good, but very large oil painting 'taking off' and coming to roost in a tree. Of course, some dealers are wizards at tying furniture down on a rack, plaiting the ties in and out of each other, and Bert could coax a set of six chairs into the back of a car, but he was exceptional.

A certain dealer was notorious for his meanness. When one day he treated me to a sandwich at a sale canteen no one would believe it. On another occasion when his car was out of action he cadged a lift from a pal who had a small van. Which made it possible for him to buy a very large marble statue which no one else cared to tackle. It must have weighed half a ton, and it took some time to load. The sale was some ten miles from his shop, and by the time it was unloaded midnight was not far away, and his perspiring pal was twenty miles from home. Now, at that time eggs were rationed, but our friend kept hens. So, to his pal he said, 'I'm very grateful to you. How would you like a dozen eggs?' 'That's very good of you, and I'd be very obliged to you.' A paper bag was found and the eggs handed over. 'Now, that'll be two and ninepence!' The story was repeated for years, but strange to say, the friendship lasted. There's a tale to be told about every dealer. One had the reputation of being a ladies' man, though he was getting on in years. It appears that some years before I knew him he was on holiday with his wife at the seaside, and one fine afternoon he escaped and met a most charming girl on the beach. The upshot was that they hired a Li-Lo and paddled a little out to sea to bathe, leaving their clothes at a bathing-hut. It was very hot, and they fell asleep. Two hours later, as it proved, they awoke to find they had drifted out to sea, and the coast was only just in sight. Luckily for them the sea was very calm, and even luckier that before very long a pleasure-trip launch took them aboard. It was not so lucky, though, that the launch landed them at a place five miles away from their clothes. I sometimes thought that this little mishap was reason enough for the utterly despondent look on his face whenever he did business.

I wish I could remember the countless tales that were told on our long journeys to sales. They alone would fill a book. Here is one that I do recall, and that I believe to be perfectly true. A pair of local dealers of very dubious reputation once heard about a very good, early chair in a nearby country cottage. Everyone had tried to buy it, but in vain, for the old woman who owned it was a very tough nut. One day they set out with a hand-cart, dressed up to the nines, and knocked at her door. When she opened the door, 'We're from the County Council, madam, and we're investigating the wood-worm pest. Can we examine your furniture?' In they went, and in due course came to the chair. 'Oh, dear! This is very badly infested! Sorry, madam, but we shall have to take it away and burn it!' Dismay and general confusion. 'Look here, madam, tell you what, we'll compensate you for it. How about ten shillings?' Ten shillings it was, and off they went with the chair on the hand-cart.

Nowadays, what with 'Going for a Song' and a general interest in antiques, the trade finds it difficult to buy goods privately even if they bid the earth. All the geese are swans. 'We saw a piece just like it on T.V., and Mr. Negus said it was worth so-and-so.' And only the rarity, recognized only by a specialist expert, goes cheaply at a sale. On the other hand there's luck. Some have it and others haven't, and I firmly believe that it is a very real, concrete phenomenon, and the cause of many a large fortune. If the dealer I refer to reads this he'll know who I mean. At a big sale one day he managed to take home a large Georgian rent table, round, with the usual drawers all around, and labelled with the letters of the alphabet. In the centre was a large metal bowl, as black as ink, into which tenants used to throw their rent. It was easily prised out and cleaned, and turned out to be silver, worth many times the value of the table. The same dealer was returning home from an abortive Black Country sale one day, and noticed a small pedestal desk standing on the pavement outside a junk-shop. He pulled up, and walked across to have a look, and out came the shirt-sleeved proprietor. 'How much d'ye want for this old desk?' 'Nice thing, ain't it? A good piece of Victorian, that is. You can 'ave it for ten quid.' He did, too, and it was Queen Anne walnut, and worth in those days over two hundred pounds. I can only remember one real piece of luck of that sort happening to me, and that was at a Sotheby sale. A small desk of the same kind came up, varnished all over with some kind of treacly goo, and with a sizeable piece of the corner of one drawer completely missing. I bought it for £68 and thought there might be ten pounds profit in it if I discounted the work I would have to do on it. I could not even tell of what wood it was made, though it had some kind of wide cross-banding. The carriers delivered it the following week, and I set to work. All the drawers were locked, but luckily I managed to find a key which opened them. In one of the drawers was the piece missing from the broken drawer, which went back into place as though it had never been off. The treacle came off fairly easily, and there beneath it was beautifully figured walnut, and cross-banding in pear-wood. To cap it all, and really to make my day, the brasses were all original.

Of course, we still hope, but nowadays usually in vain. The trouble is that the idea still persists that dealers buy for shillings and sell for as many pounds. Too many customers (and especially the rich ones) expect and ask for pounds to be taken off marked prices, not realizing that those pounds represent the profit. I sometimes wonder, and am often tempted to inquire, whether they take the same attitude in any other kind of shop.

Twelve

IN the antiques trade there are many ways of earning a living, and the beginner has to make up his mind which one to choose. At the bottom of the ladder is the junk dealer who keeps little more than a second-hand shop. If by chance he comes across anything worth while he asks more for it than a Bond Street dealer would expect to get. Some deal only in 'small stuff,' pottery, china, copper and brass, prints, and so on, and others only in furniture. Some specialize and others have a general stock. There is the dealer who caters for the trade and sells pieces in the rough that want money spent on them, while another stocks only pieces in perfect condition, properly restored if necessary, and ready to be put straight into a room, not out of place in any company. And nowadays we have more and more dealers who deal only in goods to be sold for export, and who have to keep always up to date with changing demand, whether it be for Loo tables, long-case clocks, Victorian oil-lamps, or Dutch marquetry. After long consideration I made a start in my single room having decided to depend mainly on private trade, and to offer only pieces in fine state, displayed to the best advantage, and always well-polished and free from dust.

Many collectors have become dealers, especially since antiques have become so popular and apparently profitable to sell. Some have fallen by the wayside, because once having sold their initial stock, carefully gathered together over the years, they find it impossible to replace it. They know neither how nor where to buy. A small but very important decision has to be made regarding price ticketing. Dealers of the old school are often horrified at the idea of marking up goods in plain figures, and have their private codes which are jealously guarded. I mentioned Pease of Nottingham early in this book, and told of how he made me free of his, which incidentally was WPANTIQUES, standing for the numerals 1 to 0. For my own part I remembered my own feelings of embarrassment when, feeling like a pauper, I had to ask the price of piece after piece, and I know that there is always a lurking suspicion that the use of a code may mean a fixing of prices according to the cost of a customer's car or clothes! With these thoughts in mind I adopted the system I have used ever since, the price in plain figures together with the trade price in code on the one side of the label, and on the other a short description of the piece. Other advantages apart, one can then go away and leave a customer to look around undisturbed, being readily available if more information be desired.

As time passed many kind people who had read my books found me out and came to see me. I did my best to sell them what they wanted at a reasonable price, and as a result of their recommendation my one showroom overflowed into two, then into three, and finally over the whole of the ground floor of our large house. Looking back I can see that it takes many years to become really well known if one's shop is off one of the main 'trade routes.' Trade and private customers prefer in common to visit places where a number of shops are clustered together. I was extremely fortunate in being elected a member of B.A.D.A. within a comparatively short time. Two well-established dealers came to see my stock, no one blackballed me, and in due course along came my member's certificate and round, glass emblem. Some dealers see no advantage in membership, but it is a fact that there are many who will buy only from those whose names appear among the five hundred-odd listed in the Association's little white, blue and gold book. One of my friends, having fine premises in a Cotswolds mecca of antique hunters, lost the sale of a really lovely desirable piece of furniture, offered at a very reasonable figure, when his customer found out that he 'was not B.A.D.A.'

In the beginning, when a week or more passed without a single sale, we were despondent, and saw bankruptcy staring us in the face. And then, invariably and out of the blue, would come a customer who would spend several hundreds. With customers appearances are deceptive. A man dressed like a tramp, with patches on his elbows and the seat out of his pants, can be a Lord. One of my close colleagues has a notice in his shop which reads something like this. 'If we have a piece which is just like the one your grandmother has, only hers is much better, we charge you double.' I think when he composed it he was thinking of the 'browser.' 'We only want to come in and browse' is an opening gambit which must be deeply engraved on antique dealers' hearts. To be followed in due course by the remark, as the browser takes his leave, 'You have some lovely things, but I shall have to wait until Ernie comes up!' Of course, browsers do sometimes make a purchase, but with rare exceptions an antique shop to them is a museum, a place to shelter in on a wet day, or a quiet, handy refuge in which to hold long and intimate conversations about Aunt Eliza's arthritis. There is really no need for a casual customer to make any excuse for not buying. After all, how can he know if there is anything he wants until he has looked around? A pleasant 'Thank you for letting me look round, I'll call again if I may,' is so much more genuine than 'What I was REALLY looking for was a Fabergé Easter Egg' (or an Elizabethan whatnot, or a Worcester figure of a gardener, or anything else which it is quite certain you would never have in stock). On the other hand, it is common for a genuine customer to come looking for a particular article and to go away happily with something quite different! We all know the customer who falls in love with an article and cannot make up his mind whether to buy it. He calls in a few days later, and nine times out of ten it has gone. Even if you've had it in stock for months without anyone having shown the slightest interest.

I can never quite make up my mind whether salesmanship is a desirable asset in a dealer. One can so easily appear to overpraise an article, and so to give the impression that it is a 'sticker' which must be sold at all costs! I know one dealer whose favourite remark is, 'It's for buttons!' On the whole I think that high-quality goods sell themselves, though of course a little judicious pointing out of good points, rare features and so forth does no harm. My wife Muriel is a far better salesman than I, which to her disadvantage makes me eager to leave her in charge. But then, I think that she derives as much gratification as I do myself when, on my return home after a day on the road, I am greeted with, 'I've sold quite a nice lot of things today, and the cheques are on your desk!' The truth is that without her we could not carry on, for a single-handed concern is almost impossible; one cannot be out hunting for stock and at the same time keep open all day and every day. I know from my collecting days that it is important to do this, for living as we do miles from any other comparable shop we cannot expect customers to make special journeys without being certain that we shall be open when they arrive. Because Muriel will never except at times of illness allow our premises to be closed, but is always happy and willing to put our business before her own convenience and pleasure, I have never had to contend with this problem.

Why do people pay more at a sale for an article than they would for the same thing in a dealer's shop? Not only private customers, but the trade as well? I remember offering a pair of very fine Worcester First Period hexagonal vases and covers, painted in underglaze blue, to a well-known specialist. They were too dear. Yet not so long afterwards, when the private customer who had bought them put them into a famous sale-room, the same dealer paid several hundreds of pounds more for them. Why? If a piece bought under the hammer proves later to be worm-eaten, cracked, or otherwise unsatisfactory there is no redress, whereas a reputable dealer stands by his invoice, which is a guarantee. I know that it is often said that there's no sense in paying a dealer's profit when he can be outbid in the sale-room, but it is often forgotten that his price includes the benefit of his knowledge and experience, his guarantee, and the endless time, trouble and expense he has expended in the finding of his stock.

In an earlier chapter I spoke of my old Grammar School headmaster 'Georgie' Ashe, who taught me both to paint and, I hope, to write passable English. He gave me also a love for water-colours and their painters which over the years I had developed by much study. One day my friend Hamish mentioned a certain gentleman, living not far from my home, who collected Victorian glass and was always pleased to show it. I rang up and made an appointment. Thus began yet another lasting friendship made through a common love for beautiful things. Glass he certainly had, cabinets of it all beautiful and glowing, and to my surprise, as he talked, as technically fascinating as porcelain. But that was not all, for around the walls of his rooms hung dozens of fine water-colours, which he had studied and collected for years. There were more in the bedrooms, under the staircase, and piled (or 'buried,' as he put it) in the attics. What was the more interesting I cannot tell, the glass, the water-colours, or Albert and his wife Daisy, who knows almost as much as he does. Albert himself, a hard-headed yet jovial Black Countryman, amazingly knowledgeable about so many things, was my friend from that moment. What was more, he helped me to gather together a collection of water-colours, in which I have specialized ever since.

Why are people who love antiques themselves such nice people? Meeting so many of them has been our greatest joy and our greatest reward throughout our dealing. So many invitations to see collections, so many to spend week-ends, it would take a lifetime to accept them all. It was not long after we set up in business that Gwyneth and Godfrey did the same in Ludlow, a bare nineteen miles away up and over the Clee Hills. Godfrey was a solicitor, recovering from illness, and intending to set up a practice in the quiet country town. They found a suitable house, and to occupy her time Gwyneth decided to set up a small antiques business. Collecting fine antiques had been their delight for many years. The outcome was very different, as I could have told them. The town lost a lawyer, and gained an antique shop. Our ideas of dealing ran on parallel lines, and early every Friday morning as regular as clockwork I went to Ludlow and we had coffee round the kitchen table, which was usually piled with the finds of the day before. I suppose that if we had never paid for the goods we bought from each other, there would not have been a ten-pound note in it, at the end of the year! Soon after began our annual holidays together, some of which had their moments. One day in Granada we found a gift shop which sold alabaster vases of all shapes and sizes at ridiculously low prices. Godfrey had one of his bright ideas. Why not buy a few hundredweights of them, get them shipped home, and retire on the proceeds? Or something to that effect. Followed by another bright idea. Perhaps they were made locally, and if they were, why not find out where, and buy them wholesale? The shopkeeper, so far as we could understand him, was very obliging. Yes, the vases were indeed made in the city, though he did not quite know where, because he was only the assistant, and his master was out of town. Out we marched and held a committee meeting in the street. Why not ask a policeman? The only one in sight was on traffic duty at a very busy place where five main roads met, all teeth and white pith helmet. We dodged the traffic and stood in front of him. After several minutes he stopped blowing his whistle and bent down from his little platform to see what we wanted. He spoke no English, and we no Spanish. As usual in like cases I took out my pocket-book and drew a picture of a two-handled vase, the while he looked on interestedly and the traffic hooted and snarled itself up as far as the Alhambra. He looked at my drawing for a long minute, prodded it, and suddenly grinned from ear to ear. He stepped down from his platform and commanded, I suppose, 'Follow me!' Whereupon he marched off, leaving the traffic to sort itself out as best it could, and off we set, quite clearly (in the plain opinion of the now dense crowd of spectators) under close arrest. We must have walked a mile, all self-conscious and perspiring freely. A hooting crowd of small boys followed in the rear, now and then darting forward to smile encouragement in our guilty faces. At long last our guide halted, grinned even more widely, and pointed triumphantly to the window of a large shop. Inside was a remarkably fine display of marble gravestones, angels, and marble urns. Two-handled, of course. Needless to say, we never imported any alabaster.

One of the privileges enjoyed by a dealer is to be entrusted with the forming of a collection. One day a gentleman called in to look at porcelain. We had never met, although he lived in a large house only a few miles away, where I had attended a sale of surplus furnishings years before, at the time when he had inherited the estate. Would I care to go along and look at a few pieces he had, including he thought some Worcester blue and white? A few days later I did so, and Tom, as I will call him, showed me round the house. It was a very fine building though somewhat dilapidated, and inside was much fine furniture and some fine paintings. Not to mention what seemed to be a family of enormous dogs who seemed not to take very kindly to antique dealers. The idea, it seemed, was that the house was shortly to be renovated, and the china properly displayed. Tom opened a large door at one end of the hall, and when we had entered switched on a light which hardly penetrated the far corners of an enormous, oak-panelled room, its windows fast shuttered. Several large glazed china cabinets thrust above piles of broken furniture and discarded furnishings of all kinds. We opened the doors of these and sorted out the contents, services, jugs, plates, and china ornaments of every kind. As he thought, there were some pieces of Worcester blue and white, some good Oriental, and a lot of nondescript Staffordshire ware. We talked and he grew interested. The upshot was that he felt he should have more Worcester porcelain, only coloured, not blue and white. Out of this chance visit to my shop grew a friendship and a fine collection, all choice pieces, some bought on commission at Sothebys, some from my stock, all tastefully displayed in cabinets and all, to Tom's gratification, increasing in value year by year. There has only ever been one anxiety. 'Now, are you quite sure you are asking me enough?'

We used to go to Wigan quite often, especially after the motor road made the journey easier. Jim and Mary loved coloured Worcester, and their son Joe preferred early blue and white. They already had good collections, and when they bought from me there was only one problem. It usually went something like this. Mary saw a piece she liked. 'What do you think, Jim?' 'Well, my dear, if you think you REALLY like it, but . . .' Away they would go, and sure enough, the same evening the telephone would ring. Mary had won. How rare it is for a husband and wife to agree in an antique shop! And how frustrating it is for a dealer (especially at the end of a bad week) when one of the two cribs what seems to be a certain sale! Of course there are exceptions. Particularly adoring helpmeets (especially if newly married) do sometimes say, 'If YOU like it, dear, of course we'll have it.' Or, as a husband said only last week, 'Well, my dear, whether you like it or not, I do, and I'm going to have it!' We shall have no more postponed purchases by Mary, for Jim died last year, his cabinets are full enough, and part of yet another valued friendship has ended.

I first met Celia and Charles Taylor when they came to see if I had any Worcester porcelain decorated in 'dry blue.' Apparently they were flower-growers owning a lovely nursery garden near Bridgnorth, and it was their delight not only to collect this lovely ware, but also to identify some of the forgotten flowers so accurately painted upon it, and even to try to reintroduce them into their beds for their own pleasure and that of their customers. Since that day I have had the pleasure of finding many pieces for them, and their collection, beautifully set out in pastel-shaded alcoves, is a joy to see. Charles is a large and forceful ex-Army Major, and as becomes a horticulturist he is wont to call a spade a spade. When I go to see them I usually find these kind-hearted, gentle people side by side, planting and delving, and I never cease to marvel how Charles's large and powerful hands can possibly hold a flower so tenderly, or fail to crush a piece of their lovely, fragile ware.

I suppose it was because my first book was about a kind of porcelain that was not widely popular that so many wrote to me, thanking me for writing it. One correspondent said it helped him to recover from his stroke, and gave him another kind of disease. He cured it by starting to collect blue and white, but the bug is still intermittently virulent. It is good to know that many of his best pieces came from me, and a day spent with him and his wife, and their three sons (and the peacocks making hideous the country air outside) is always something to remember. I had a letter one day from a lady living in North Wales, asking me to send her a copy of one of my books. I did so, and by return came her cheque, with thanks because I had trusted her. I thought nothing more of it, until some time later I had a local telephone call from a hotel in the town. The name was Jolliffe and we had never met.

He was the husband of the lady to whom I had sent my book, and would my wife and I care to join them at dinner that evening? So started another firm friendship. Not only were Barry and Janet keen collectors (particularly, on her part, of New Hall) but he was a keen fisherman, and had a lake of his own up in the hills behind Llanbedr, ten miles away from Conway on the Bettws-y-Coed road. Also, he was a talented amateur painter in oils. What more could we have in common? Since that day my wife and I, or I alone, have spent many refreshing days at the whitewashed house that was once an inn, where Ibbetson once worked for a short space, and opposite the other inn where David Cox stayed and which he illustrated in a letter to a friend. I count among my fondest memories the quiet evenings seated around the great open fireplace, talking of this and that, or silent in the best kind of comradeship, or looking at the television until Barry falls asleep in uncomprehending boredom. I think he will not mind if I mention that my early visits had only one kind of disappointment. Fishes did not like living in his lake.

So I could go on. Customers become friends, and many fine pieces which one is so loath to sell find homes where one can still, from time to time, admire them once more.

Thirteen

THINKING back over the years on the eve of my retirement I can see how collecting has changed; the better because I can see it from both sides of the fence, as it were. The time was when like all collectors I lived in a little world of my own particular interest, whereas now I have to be interested in a great many things, and can see how the scene is continually changing. The collector is no longer the oddity he was once thought to be because the interest in the old and beautiful is so widespread. Young folk about to set up house do not always rush to the modern furniture store but are happy to pick up their pieces gradually, as they can afford them, at sales or at antique shops. Older couples often wait until their children have left them, and replace their old, scratched and dented Edwardian furniture with something they now realize is more worth while. And hardly a day passes but a customer remarks to me, 'When I think of the things we gave away when my father died!' Why this change, all within the last few years?

Undoubtedly I suppose that the B.B.C. has a lot to answer for. And perhaps to be proud of. Like Pygmalion, my old friend Arthur Negus little knew what he was starting. At any rate, his programme has put antiques before the public. Everyone is 'antique conscious,' and because he puts it over so well the course of instruction is quite painless. I know that not all dealers approve of the buying public knowing so much, or at any rate thinking that they do, but anything that brings customers is good for trade in the long run. Add to 'Going for a Song' the opening of stately homes to the public, the increasing number of weekly newspapers dealing with collecting, and the publication of books by people like me, and it is easy to see why collecting is so popular.

In some ways I think it has gone mad, though it is not perhaps in the best interests of a dealer to say so. Who would have thought, a few years ago, that anyone would value, let alone treasure and pay big money for, Stevengraphs, pot-lids, or German fairings? Or even for a chamber-pot to put flowers in and stand upon the sideboard? The magnificent specimen with a coloured picture of an open-mouthed Napoleon Bonaparte in the bottom, which I saw at Broadway, was of course a rarity. And in passing, has anyone ever seen a Hitler version?

Is the truth of the matter that folk no longer have any trust in money? Fine pieces have always commanded high prices, some of them even higher than now, but there is I think more to it than a mere searching for possible profitable or even likely secure means of investment. Is it not possible that hitherto unconsidered trifles have been deliberately 'promoted'? Are collectors and the trade alike being taken in by gimmicks?

These are questions I cannot try to answer, but I do know that sale prices, and the questions I am often asked about possible appreciation of things which I sell, indicate that a new kind of collector has appeared, who often has no interest in antiques other than monetary, though it is at the same time gratifying to know that many who buy as a safe investment grow to love their new possessions for their own sake.

Time was when an antique shop was popularly looked upon as a kind of Holy of Holies, to be entered with bated breath by well-breeched connoisseurs. Almost, one expected to be asked to leave one's shoes outside the door. That is all changed for the better. But at the same time many sources of supply in the trade are somewhat dubious. A friend of mine was called by telephone the other day to see some goods at a private house. He deals in small stuff, and there was quite a lot of it. To make a start, 'What will you take for this part Pratt dessert-service?' '£150.' 'And this pair of George I brass sticks?' They were £45. 'Too dear for me, I'm afraid.' 'But they're worth it!' 'Even if they were,' said my friend, 'I'm in business to make a living, and I have to make a profit. I'm afraid you're wasting your time and mine.' Of course, as soon as he entered the room he knew that the woman was in business as a dealer, though pretending to be a private owner. There are many like her, knowing little about antiques and less of values, but eager to jump on the band wagon of the antiques boom. They expect to be quoted trade prices, and usually ask their customers what was written on the original ticket, plus a little extra. They are neither fish nor fowl, but strange to say many of them are held in higher repute than a genuine trader.

What is the future of Fairs? We all know that nowhere in the world can so many fine antiques be seen under one roof as at the original Grosvenor House Antiques Fair, and a number of established provincial Fairs are almost as good. On the other hand there are many at which the standard is very low, partly because the 'vetting' is too slack, and partly because the slackly enforced date limits allow much to be offered that is not even antique in the accepted sense of the word. It is most noticeable that at some of these Fairs hardly a single well-known, established dealer has a stand, and that in consequence hardly a good piece of Georgian or even Regency furniture is to be seen. We know that even Edwardian furniture is often extremely well-made and handsome, but the time to offer it at an Antiques Fair is not yet. At the same time I would be the last person to suggest that there is any intention to deceive or to defraud, because the truth is that so many who call themselves antique dealers do not understand antiques.

Before I finish writing this book for the second time I have a confession to make. Call it vanity if you will, but I call it nostalgia, for the truth is that I often take down my old dog-eared copy and read through its pages. They bring back to me memories of events and of people I thought I had forgotten, and I relive so many cherished hours. The words I wrote in what was then my last paragraph are still as true as ever, despite a sad debasing of our lovely antique currency. I rejoice to know that in a world in which monetary values predominate there are still true collectors and dealers who are always happy to advise and to help them. I am very happy to think that I may have been counted among their number.